BREAKING DEMOCRACY'S CHAINS

Freeing and Fortifying Democracy Against

Hidden Capture

BREAKING DEMOCRACY'S CHAINS

Freeing and Fortifying Democracy Against Hidden Capture

By METIN PEKIN

Copyright © 2025, Metin Pekin.

All rights reserved. The use of any part of this publication,
reproduced, transmitted in any form or by any means, electronic,
mechanical, photocopying, recording or otherwise stored
in a retrieval system, without the prior consent of the author
is an infringement of the copyright law.

This material is protected by copyright law and may not be used
for machine learning, AI training, or data mining
without explicit written permission. This includes,
but is not limited to, the use of text, images,
and other content for the development of AI models.

First edition.

ISBN: 978-1-77849-086-6

Contents

INTRODUCTION: ... 1
Why This Book Exists—And Why It Can't Wait

CHAPTER 1   The Invisible Cage We Call Freedom   3
The Architecture of Control and the Illusion of Democracy

CHAPTER 2   The Birth of Political Parties in the USA   12
How Political Parties Streamlined Elite Control

CHAPTER 3   Defending the Indefensible   28
Debunking the Twelve Myths of Party Democracy

CHAPTER 4   The True Price of Loyalty   59
How Political Parties Fuel War, Division, and Institutional Decay

CHAPTER 5   The Politics of Division   76
How Parties Turn People Against Each Other

CHAPTER 6   Trojan Democracy   86
How Political Parties Enable Foreign Rule

CHAPTER 7   The Fourth Estate in Chains   106
Political Parties and the Death of Media Independence

CHAPTER 8   Justice Captured   127
When the Courts Serve the Powerful

Chapter 9 The Illusion of Democratic Choice 136
How Parties Hijack Representation, Silence Dissent, and Sell Us the Illusion of Freedom

Chapter 10 Political Religion 147
Worshipping the Party as a Way of Life

Chapter 11 Democracy Is a Journey, Not a Destination 164
From Parties to People: The Next Step in Democratic Evolution

Chapter 12 A Blueprint for Real Democracy 176
Designing a Responsive System for Any Economy

Chapter 13 Break the Chains, Not the System 195
Disempowering Parties by Refusing to Vote for Them

About the Author 226

Introduction

Why This Book Exists—And Why It Can't Wait

MOST PEOPLE SENSE that something is wrong with modern democracy even if they can't quite put their finger on it. They vote, they protest, they hope. But nothing fundamental ever seems to change. The rich grow richer, the wars continue, and governments of every stripe serve interests that seem far removed from the everyday citizen.

We are told this is democracy. That the ability to vote every few years for one of two or three political parties is the pinnacle of freedom. That change, if it comes at all, must come through these established channels. But what if that very structure the party system is the reason change never arrives?

This book challenges the most sacred assumption in modern politics: that political parties are essential to democracy. It argues the opposite—that they are the very mechanism by which democracy has been captured, neutralised, and sold back to the people as a polished illusion.

Drawing on history, political theory, real-world case studies, and contemporary examples, this book lays bare how party systems manufacture consent, suppress dissent, and centralise power. It also offers an alternative: a No-Party model rooted in direct accountability and genuine representation, designed not to reform or rebalance the party system but to eliminate it entirely.

Over the following chapters, we will examine how political parties distort representation, enable elite control, suppress meaningful reform, and manufacture division. But we will also explore a practical way forward—a model of No-Party democracy that restores power to the people by removing parties from the system altogether.

If you have ever felt disillusioned with politics—not because you are apathetic, but because you care too much to pretend anymore—this book is for you.

Chapter 1

The Invisible Cage We Call Freedom

The Architecture of Control and the Illusion of Democracy

Call it what you will: democracy, liberty, self-rule. Or, as more and more people have come to believe, a managed illusion, a ritual of obedience, a game rigged by the powerful. Democracy was the shining ideal sold to you since the day you could walk. You were told you lived in a free society. You were told your voice mattered. You were told that every few years, you had the power to shake the world by putting a piece of paper in a box.

And yet here you are.

Watching—year after year, election after election, promise after broken promise—and nothing fundamental ever changes. The rich grow richer. The wars rage on. The corporations grow fatter. The machinery of your daily life grinds on, indifferent to voting booths and campaign slogans.

Somewhere deep inside, a part of you already knows:

> You are not free.
> You are not even close.
> You are allowed to choose—but only between pre-approved options.

You are allowed to speak—but only within acceptable limits.
You are allowed to vote—but only to decide which servant of the elite wears the crown.

This is not democracy.

It is the theatre of democracy—a polished illusion designed to distract, not to empower.

It is freedom repackaged as ritual, participation reduced to performance.

Like Rome's 'bread and circuses', it offers just enough comfort and spectacle to keep the people quiet while the emperors rule unchallenged.

It is consent, acted out on a stage built by the powerful—scripted by their advisors, funded by their donors, and sealed off from any real escape.

You are not witnessing democracy. You are watching a play—and the audience never gets to rewrite the ending.

You live in a cage so cleverly built, it looks like the horizon.

But the exits are sealed—and the party system holds the keys.

This book is about that cage—and how to escape it.

Across the so-called democratic world—from Washington to London, from Paris to Brasília—a quiet disease festers. It's not something easily named. It's not shouted from the rooftops. It creeps in during the quiet moments. When you realise the cost of living rises but wages don't. When you watch another war justified with the same tired lies. When you see the rich bailed out, while the poor are lectured about responsibility.

It's the sick feeling after another election night.

The slow dawning horror that nothing real will happen.

The sense that no matter who wins, you lose.

You feel it when you watch candidates who promised hope morph overnight into servants of the same old interests. You feel it when the media tells you with a straight face that this time is different—and somehow, you know it's not. You sense, even if you can't yet fully articulate it, that democracy has become a charade. An endless loop of excitement, outrage, hope, despair, and apathy—neatly recycled every few years like seasons on a television show.

And the worst part is: they want you to blame each other.

> **Left blames right.**
> **Right blames left.**

Fingers point in every direction, except up, where the puppet masters pull the strings.

While you burn bridges with your friends over politics, the real rulers of your world sip champagne behind closed doors. And the machine grinds on, untouched.

Generation after generation, we've been taught to believe that political parties are the foundation of democracy. They appear everywhere—on your ballot paper, on your television, in your classrooms, in casual conversation, and carved into the walls of every institution that claims to speak for you. Red or blue. Centre or fringe. Left, right, or something in between. But what if none of them are truly working for you? What if the problem isn't the party in power, but the structure that keeps them all in place? What if the game is fixed—and changing the players changes nothing?

Political parties, we are told, are inevitable. Human nature demands them. Organised politics needs them. Stability requires them. But these assumptions go largely unchallenged. We critique policies, we debate leaders, we argue over ideologies—but rarely do we stop to ask: should political parties exist at all? Have they served the people? Or have they become the very tools by which popular power is diluted, controlled, and redirected?

The truth is stark: the party system does not serve democracy. It *subverts* it. It centralises power. It manufactures division. It packages dissent into safe, predictable channels. It builds barriers to entry for anyone unwilling to play by its rules. It ensures that real change—the kind that redistributes power, dismantles corruption, or threatens elite control—is either marginalised or neutralised before it ever reaches the ballot.

Parties are not engines of democracy. They are bottlenecks—filters built to ensure that only certain people, with certain views, ever get near real power. They exist not to serve you, but to protect themselves. Once a party gains power, its primary mission is no longer to serve the public—it is to preserve its own dominance. Dissent within the ranks is crushed. Innovation is punished. Real representation is sacrificed at the altar of party loyalty.

Elected officials do not act freely.

They are bound by the whip—forced into line by party enforcers.

Those who stray—those who dare to speak for their constituents over their party bosses—are sidelined, smeared, deselected, destroyed.

You are told these officials represent you. In truth, they answer to the donors, lobbyists, and power brokers who fund their party—and it is their interests the party must protect to survive. Party loyalty isn't about serving the public. It's about preserving the system that keeps the powerful in power.

You don't have to dig into conspiracy theories to find proof. The evidence is out in the open—and has been for decades.

In the United States, Pulitzer Prize-winning journalist Chris Hedges describes modern America as a "corporate oligarchy"—where both major parties are funded by the same banks, the same defence contractors, the same tech giants. In *Empire of Illusion* and *Death of the Liberal Class*, Hedges pulls back the curtain: elections are ritualised theatre, where the illusion of choice is maintained while corporate interests run the show behind the scenes.

Whether left or right, any political figure who threatens entrenched interests becomes a target—not of open democratic debate, but of internal sabotage, media manipulation, and increasingly, legal or institutional warfare.

In the United Kingdom, Jeremy Corbyn—twice elected as Labour leader by the party's grassroots—faced relentless sabotage not just from external opponents, but from his own party machine.

Leaked communications revealed Labour officials actively worked to lose elections under his leadership, fearing that genuine left-wing policies would threaten their cosy status quo. The media, largely owned by a handful of billionaires, waged a non-stop campaign of vilification. Military officials even hinted at mutiny should he win—a soft threat of coup dressed up in plausible deniability.

And Corbyn was not alone. On the other side of the aisle, Boris Johnson—who won a landslide general election in 2019 with the largest Conservative majority in decades—was, according to former minister Nadine Dorries, deliberately removed by internal party operatives. In her explosive book *The Plot*, Dorries alleges that a secretive faction within the Conservative Party coordinated his downfall, acting not in response to public will but to protect their own entrenched influence. Johnson, she claims, was not brought down by voters, but by insiders—a political assassination staged within the party machinery itself. When even a sitting Prime Minister with a popular mandate can be quietly pushed out by unelected actors behind closed doors, the myth of democratic control begins to collapse.

In the United States, Bernie Sanders ignited millions with promises to break corporate dominance. But in both 2016 and 2020, he faced the full resistance of the Democratic Party establishment. Leaked emails confirmed elite coordination to undermine him. In 2020, the Democratic leadership orchestrated a rapid consolidation behind Joe Biden to neutralise Sanders' momentum. The media—owned by the very corporations he aimed to challenge—treated him not as a contender, but as a threat.

Marine Le Pen—long painted as the face of the far-right in France—was formally barred from standing in future elections following her conviction for misusing EU parliamentary funds. The five-year ban from public office, upheld in 2024 and cutting her out of the 2027 presidential race, came not during a scandalous low point, but at a moment of rising support.

Whether one agrees or disagrees with her politics is beside the point. The significance lies in the pattern. As her candidacy gained serious momentum, legal and institutional mechanisms kicked into high gear. Charges that had lingered for years were suddenly pursued with full force. Her emergency appeal to the European Court of Human Rights was swiftly dismissed—sealing the ban.

This is not a defence of her ideology, but an observation of how systems respond when popular challengers—even within the electoral rules—threaten elite continuity. The charges themselves were not fabricated. But the timing, intensity, and total institutional alignment in response to her growing electoral strength suggest a political system designed not for fairness, but for containment.

You are told that democracy means choice. But what kind of choice is it when every candidate must first pass through party filters—when campaigns are funded by billionaires, corporate lobbies, and shadowy influence groups with bottomless pockets, while ordinary citizens can't afford to keep the lights on? Even well-meaning candidates are forced by their own parties to play by rules written by elites. And once elected, both major parties—supposedly bitter rivals—serve the same industries, fight the same wars, and shield the same financial elites.

What kind of choice is it when dissenting voices are systematically starved of media oxygen? When candidates who dare to challenge the system—people like Corbyn, Sanders, or grassroots independents—are smeared, sidelined, or erased from the conversation?

History has shown that the party system is no straightforward vehicle for the people's will. It is a structure refined over time to manage, channel, and ultimately contain that will—and today, it is performing that role with ruthless efficiency.

You don't live in a democracy. You live in a carefully stage-managed environment where you are herded from scandal to scandal, outrage to outrage, election to election—too exhausted to ask why the system never changes, only the actors.

At every critical moment—economic collapse, pandemic, war—the mask slips. And you see, if only for a moment, the truth that was always there:

- Banks crash the economy—and both parties rush to bail them out.
- Endless wars bleed nations dry—and both parties vote to fund them.
- Life-saving medicines remain unaffordable—and both parties protect the pharmaceutical giants who profit from your pain.
- Whistleblowers expose mass surveillance—and both parties protect the agencies that violated your rights while punishing those who told the truth.

When it comes to protecting the wealthy, when it comes to maintaining the empire of donors and lobbyists, the divisions between the major parties evaporate like mist.

They perform conflict on television.

They argue bitterly over cultural flashpoints.

They whip you into tribal rage over slogans, flags, mascots.

Meanwhile, on the things that truly matter—war, wealth, surveillance, power—they close ranks.

Every time you walk into a voting booth and select from their pre-approved list, you are participating in your own containment. You are feeding the machine that grinds you down—the same machine that distracts you with bread and circuses, divides you with tribal identity, and silences you with manufactured consent.

But it wasn't always like this. The system we see today is not the one its founders intended.

The Founding Fathers and the Rise of Political Parties: A Betrayal of the Original Vision

They feared it, but circumstances forced their hand. The American republic was not born in apathy. It was born in fire—the fire of revolution, of resistance, of an uncompromising demand for self-rule. Its architects did not imagine a perfect democracy, but they did imagine something radically different from the world they had escaped: a government accountable to its people, restrained by checks and balances, and fiercely protective of individual liberty.

Above all, the Founders feared concentrated power—and they saw political factions as its fastest route. To them, political parties were not instruments of democracy, but infections that could rot it from within. These worries were not abstract or academic. The Founding Fathers had witnessed in European history, and in their own colonial governance, how factions devoured nations from the inside—transforming public service into partisan warfare, and representation into rivalry.

John Adams saw it clearly. Writing to Jonathan Jackson in 1780, he warned: "There is nothing which I dread so much as a division of the republic into two great parties." He foresaw the likely outcome: a permanent struggle for dominance, with each side willing to sacrifice principle for power and the citizenry trapped in a false choice. In such a scenario, the people would no longer be truly sovereign; they would become spectators in a game rigged long before the first vote was cast.

George Washington, in his Farewell Address of 1796, turned his final words as President into a solemn warning. He urged Americans to *"discourage and restrain"* the spirit of party. Washington cautioned that someday political parties would allow "cunning, ambitious, and unprincipled men" to subvert the will of the people—that they would inflame divisions, manipulate fears, and take power under the false banner of representing the public interest.

Thomas Jefferson—though later a reluctant founder of a party himself—initially viewed party politics as a form of moral decline. He called parties "the bane of republican government," fearing they would cause citizens to abandon critical thought in favor of blind loyalty. In a 1789 letter to Francis Hopkinson, Jefferson lamented how partisan alignment distorted every discussion, turning cooperation into conflict and governance into theater.

James Madison, the most systematic thinker among the Founders, gave the earliest thorough analysis of factionalism in

Federalist No. 10. He acknowledged that factions—groups of people united by shared interests—were inevitable in a free society, since suppressing them would require suppressing liberty itself. His solution was to dilute their influence through scale: a large, diverse republic would make it hard for any single faction to dominate. But even Madison, in his cautious optimism, could not foresee how quickly those factions would coalesce into something new—political machines of control.

And yet, despite all these warnings, the rise of parties was not just possible—it was inevitable. Not because they were right, but because they were needed.

Political parties did not emerge out of philosophical brilliance—they arose out of practical necessity. At the time of the American Founding Fathers, the average citizen was not literate, had no access to newspapers, let alone books, and certainly no exposure to competing viewpoints from across the country. The very idea of an informed electorate was aspirational at best.

There was no television. No internet. No radio. No social media. If you wanted to run for office or share a political vision, you couldn't livestream your thoughts or post them online—you needed a network. You needed allies to help spread the message. You needed editors, printers, pamphleteers. You needed couriers, town meetings, and speeches in candlelit halls. In short, you needed a party, or you didn't stand a chance.

And so, despite the Founders' explicit warnings about the dangers of factions, parties emerged to fill the gap—not as ideal democratic institutions, but as the only viable method to navigate a fragmented, low-information society. They were not noble by design, but necessary by circumstance. But that world no longer exists.

Chapter 2

The Birth of Political Parties in the USA

How Political Parties Streamlined Elite Control

The Constitution itself, ambiguous in places and silent in others, left vast room for interpretation. The debates that followed in the new republic—about the power of the federal government, the role of a national bank, taxation, debt, and America's place in the world—were not minor quibbles. They were existential questions for the young nation. And when power is up for grabs in a system with no formal parties, informal factions will eventually create them.

Alexander Hamilton, ever the champion of a strong central authority, rallied like-minded leaders into what became known as the Federalist camp. They argued for a robust national government, closer ties with Britain, and an economy built on industry and finance. In opposition, Thomas Jefferson and James Madison organised their followers around a vision of agrarian democracy, strong states' rights, and a strict interpretation of the Constitution. The lines were drawn—not officially, but unmistakably. And once drawn, those lines hardened into machinery.

By the late 1790s, these opposing factions had evolved into America's first political parties. The Federalists and the

Democratic-Republicans began behaving not as philosophical societies or mere coalitions of principle, but as competing organizations geared to win—seeking to control government appointments, pass or block legislation, and dominate the flow of information to the public. What had begun as spirited debate over policy turned into calculated warfare for power.

And with that party machinery came the instinct to suppress opposition.

In 1798, with the Federalists briefly in power, Congress passed the infamous Alien and Sedition Acts—four laws ostensibly aimed at national security. In practice, they became a partisan weapon used to silence journalists, immigrants, and political opponents aligned with Jefferson's camp. One of these acts made it a crime to publish *"false, scandalous, and malicious writing"* against the government—language so broad it could criminalize nearly any criticism of those in power. The First Amendment, barely a decade old, was already under siege by partisan fervor.

The public backlash to these excesses was fierce. In the presidential election of 1800, Thomas Jefferson defeated incumbent Federalist John Adams. Jefferson's victory was celebrated as a triumph of true republicanism—the first peaceful transfer of power between opposing political factions in American history. But beneath that celebratory moment lay a deeper, more troubling shift. The party system—warned against, feared, and adamantly rejected by the Founders—had nevertheless been *legitimized*. It was no longer an aberration or a temporary expedient. It was becoming the new architecture of American governance.

From that point forward, no candidate could rise to high office without party backing. No major policy could be enacted without party coordination. Hardly any dissent could be voiced in government without risking punishment from party leaders. The system designed in Philadelphia for independent representatives, each accountable to their constituents, was quickly morphing into a partisan machine—one that demanded loyalty to the party organization above loyalty to the people those representatives served.

Over time, those early Federalist and Republican factions metastasized into today's Democratic and Republican parties. The names and specific ideologies would shift over the centuries, but the basic structure—the two-party framework—never changed. The two-party system became a duopoly: a self-reinforcing gatekeeper that decides who gets to run for office, what ideas are considered "acceptable" for debate, and which policies are allowed to reach the public agenda.

Through it all, the illusion of popular freedom persisted. Yes, Americans still voted. Yes, they still chose their leaders. But only from among two pre-selected options—both vetted, funded, and constrained by the party apparatus long before any public vote. Any candidate who deviated too far from the accepted script was quietly buried by a lack of funding, smeared by partisan media, or simply locked out of the debates entirely.

This was not the future the Founders had envisioned. And yet it was the future their decisions, through necessity and historical circumstance, helped to create. Not out of malice, but out of confusion and fear during a fragile time, they made compromises that ultimately enabled the very outcome they dreaded. Lacking stronger protections against factional control, they found themselves inadvertently building the system they once condemned.

Now, more than two centuries later, the machinery the Founders warned against has grown into something more formidable than even they could have imagined. It has become a self-sustaining illusion of democracy.

It didn't begin with deception; it began with fear. Fear of instability, of disunity, of a young republic collapsing under the weight of its own contradictions. In trying to hold the nation together, the early leaders eventually embraced the very tools they once vowed to avoid.

You've been told that political parties are the lifeblood of democracy—that they help organise governance, mobilise voters, and provide stability. That without them, democratic systems would descend into chaos or gridlock. But peel back the surface, and a different picture emerges.

What follows is not a theoretical critique, but a forensic examination of how the party system—especially in the United States—has become the primary delivery mechanism for elite dominance. It is a story of how democracy became a commodity, how influence was monetised, and how control was centralised behind the comforting rituals of ballots, flags, and campaign ads.

In today's electoral landscape, money is not simply influence—it is admission. Success in politics demands financial firepower. Campaigns are no longer modest affairs; presidential races in the United States now cost billions. Political parties don't resist this trend—they depend on it. They have evolved into brokers of access—not just to the electorate, but to the institutions of power itself.

Once corporate and billionaire capital becomes embedded in the party infrastructure, the system begins to reflect the priorities of funders, not voters. Representation is reduced to spectacle. Legislation becomes transactional. And elected officials, dependent on party machines for funding and future advancement, quickly learn that defying donor interests is a fast track to political exile.

Policy, once debated and deliberated, is now shaped by negotiation—not with the public, but with financiers. The cost of this arrangement is the slow suffocation of public voice.

Popular priorities—from affordable healthcare and climate action to workers' rights and meaningful accountability—are drowned out by lobbyist agendas and donor-approved talking points.

The rise of "dark money"—political spending from undisclosed sources—has accelerated this transformation. But the rot set in long before.

The story begins in the early 20th century, as American industrialists amassed enormous fortunes and sought ways to safeguard their influence. Foundations like the Rockefeller Foundation, established in 1913, became vehicles for turning charitable giving into strategic dominance. When Congress introduced the federal charitable-contribution deduction just four years later, such donations became tax-advantaged, reducing burdens for the ultra-wealthy while enabling them to shape policy, education, research, and public discourse, all without public oversight. The ink was barely dry on these institutions' charters before the tax code began rewarding them.

These foundations became the early vehicles of elite control: polished façades for the laundering of influence. Their model was soon replicated across the political spectrum. Think tanks multiplied. Political contributions became more sophisticated, more cloaked, and more coordinated.

Jane Mayer's *Dark Money* reveals how billionaire networks—notably those led by Charles and David Koch—used their wealth to infiltrate every layer of the democratic system. From elections and academia to media and public policy, the Koch network and its allies created an infrastructure designed not to compete in open debate, but to dominate it.

They didn't simply support candidates. They funded the environments that produced them. They created the narratives that justified their policy agenda. And they cloaked their efforts in anonymity to avoid accountability.

Their influence was systematic, not sporadic. Strategic, not opportunistic. And long-term, not fleeting. The result? A distortion of democracy so profound that public consensus on critical issues—like environmental protection, healthcare, and taxation—could be overridden at will by unelected billionaires.

And then came the final blow to electoral integrity: Citizens United.

If dark money laid the groundwork, the Supreme Court's 2010 decision in *Citizens United v. FEC* poured concrete over the foundation. The Court declared that corporations, as associations of individuals, have First Amendment rights—and that limiting their ability to spend money on political messaging was an unconstitutional restriction of free speech. The ruling conflated money with speech and corporations with people.

Suddenly, there were no meaningful limits on what corporations and ultra-wealthy individuals could spend to influence elections.

Super PACs (independent political action committees) became the new currency of power—able to raise and spend unlimited sums with no requirement to disclose their donors.

The numbers are staggering. In the 2016 U.S. federal elections, an estimated $6.5 billion was spent, only slightly below the record $7 billion spent in 2012. A disproportionate share came from a few hundred ultra-wealthy donors, many with close ties to the Republican Party. The spending of this small elite rivalled—and in some cases exceeded—the combined contributions of millions of ordinary citizens.

These donors don't just shape campaigns. They decide which candidates are viable before the public ever sees a debate stage. Those who align with donor interests are elevated. Those who diverge are defunded and dismissed. And once in office, these candidates understand the unspoken contract: deliver for the donors—or be replaced.

Few names are as closely associated with the corruption of American democracy as the Koch brothers. They did not merely donate to candidates or causes—they constructed a parallel infrastructure for permanent political influence.

Their apparatus spanned think tanks, political action committees, advocacy organisations, academic institutions, and media channels—all promoting an ultra-libertarian ideology: hostility to taxation, regulation, environmental protections, and collective bargaining. But unlike traditional donors, the Koch network operated on a different scale. They didn't seek influence over a single bill or candidate. They aimed to reshape the political terrain itself.

Through tax-exempt charities, opaque funding structures, and an ever-expanding list of front groups, the Kochs funneled hundreds of millions into America's political bloodstream—always staying just out of sight. Their donations were not charity; they were strategic investments. And the returns were extraordinary.

Candidates aligned with Koch interests were showered with campaign support, third-party endorsements, and media amplification. Those who dared to oppose their agenda were punished: denied funding, targeted by primary challengers, or attacked by anonymous PAC ads. Party loyalty—particularly within the GOP—began to mean loyalty to the Koch network.

What followed was not merely legislative influence, but a policy revolution engineered from the top down:

- Deregulation of key sectors, particularly energy and finance
- Massive tax cuts for corporations and the ultra-wealthy
- Union suppression and dismantling of collective bargaining rights
- Defunding of public services and watchdog agencies

All of it carried out under the banner of "freedom," "efficiency," and "free enterprise." All of it made palatable by think tanks, media pundits, and politicians trained to speak in polished, donor-approved language.

Jane Mayer's investigations show how the Koch network bypassed democratic mechanisms altogether. They didn't need to control every elected official. They only needed to control the gatekeepers—committee chairs, party leaders, and key legislative strategists. Once those levers were captured, the rest of Congress would fall into line.

But elite influence in U.S. politics didn't begin with Super PACs. Its roots lie in an older and more entrenched system: lobbying. What began as informal persuasion has grown into a professionalised, institutionalised industry that drafts legislation, guides regulation, and controls entire policy areas.

The origins stretch back to the Gilded Age, when robber barons realised they could protect their wealth not just through competition, but through legislation. As government grew, so did their need to influence it. And thus was born the modern lobbyist—the middleman between money and power.

By the early 20th century, lobbying had matured into a core function of corporate strategy. The Sherman Antitrust Act (1890) and Clayton Act (1914), passed to limit monopolies, triggered an arms race in influence. Corporations began embedding themselves in the legislative process, not reacting to laws but shaping them from inception.

This evolution reached a turning point in the 1970s. Lewis Powell—a corporate lawyer who would soon become a Supreme Court Justice—authored a now-infamous memo warning America's business elite that they were losing the ideological war. His solution? Seize back control by saturating academia, media, and policymaking institutions with pro-business thought.

From that memo sprang an entire ecosystem of influence. Lobbying firms, legal consultants, research centres, and "nonpartisan" policy shops proliferated. By the 21st century, lobbying had become a $3.8 billion industry. But the money tells only part of the story. The real advantage was structural: lobbying became inseparable from governance itself.

Corporations didn't need to lobby every legislator. They only needed to capture the party leaders and committee chairs. And thanks to the centralised structure of political parties, this was not only possible—it was efficient.

Instead of persuading hundreds of independent lawmakers with diverse priorities, lobbyists can focus their efforts on a handful of gatekeepers. Party leaders control committee assignments. Party whips enforce discipline. Fundraising is centralised. Messaging is coordinated.

In exchange for campaign contributions, lobbyists receive two critical assets: access and agenda control.

Think tanks provide white papers. PACs bundle donations. Industry consultants meet with legislative staff. And when bills are introduced, they already contain pre-written clauses from the corporate world—often inserted with no public scrutiny.

In recent years, federal lobbying has consistently exceeded $4 billion annually, with pharmaceutical companies alone accounting for billions more—often dwarfing the capacity of consumer advocacy groups. As a result, corporate agendas often set the terms of policy debate before the public even has a voice.

Within this structure, political parties do not mediate between the public and the state. They mediate between donors and lawmakers. The will of the people becomes just one factor in a complex equation—and often, it is the most easily ignored.

Every time the public gets a glimpse of this machinery, a predictable cycle unfolds: outrage, regulation, adaptation. Laws are passed to limit money in politics. Loopholes are found. Influence finds a new disguise.

The elite do not fear regulation. They plan for it.

Take the Federal Election Campaign Act (FECA) of the 1970s and the Bipartisan Campaign Reform Act (BCRA) of 2002. Both were hailed as landmark efforts to curb political corruption. Both were gutted by lawyers, loopholes, and legal precedent.

With the rise of Super PACs, 501(c)(4) social welfare groups, and independent expenditure vehicles, donors retained—and in many cases *expanded*—their ability to shape elections without public scrutiny. The Citizens United and McCutcheon rulings completed the demolition job, effectively enshrining the right of the wealthy to drown out ordinary voices.

Tax codes are written with ambiguity that only the wealthiest can afford to navigate. Regulations are delayed, softened, or quietly rewritten by captured agencies. And perhaps most devastating of all: public servants are groomed for private sector roles—ensuring future access in exchange for present obedience.

This is not corruption in the traditional sense. It is systemic capture. And it thrives in the shadow of party power.

In this captured system, the line between public office and private power has all but disappeared. Lawmakers and regulators routinely leave government only to reappear months later as lobbyists, consultants, or board members for the very industries they once oversaw. This is known as the revolving door.

For corporations, this is the perfect strategy. Why fight regulation when you can simply hire the people who write it?

Brody Mullins, in *The Wolves of K Street*, documents this in chilling detail. Former regulators who once imposed rules on Wall Street soon join the very banks they regulated. Congressional staffers who helped draft pharmaceutical legislation land jobs with drug companies. Lawmakers who once led oversight committees resurface as lobbyists with direct access to their former colleagues. This isn't corruption in the form of envelopes of cash. It's corruption embedded in career planning.

And it's global. After resigning as UK Prime Minister, David Cameron joined Greensill Capital, a shadowy finance firm later embroiled in scandal. He reportedly stood to make £10 million, lobbying former colleagues in government to benefit his new employer.

Tony Blair, once the face of "New Labour," amassed a vast post-office fortune advising Gulf monarchies, authoritarian regimes, and multinational corporations—many of whom benefited from the deregulated global order he helped entrench.

In the United States, Barack Obama signed a multi-year production deal with Netflix reportedly worth tens of millions, accepted speaking engagements with Wall Street firms for around $400,000 a speech, and joined the leadership advisory team of a private equity-backed venture.

And in Germany, Gerhard Schröder crossed perhaps the boldest line: after shaping German energy policy as Chancellor, he took the helm of Nord Stream's shareholders' committee, a pipeline venture majority-owned by Gazprom. In 2022, Gazprom nominated him to its board—a move so politically toxic after Russia's invasion of Ukraine that he was forced to withdraw. Even without the title, Schröder has remained a lightning rod for criticism over his close ties to Russian energy interests.

Politicians, knowing they may soon depend on future corporate roles, learn to avoid antagonising the industries that may one day employ them. Lobbying firms offer premium salaries to former public officials because they bring more than policy knowledge—they bring relationships, credibility, and access that money alone can't buy.

This system operates across both major parties. It is not ideological. It is structural. And because party leadership controls committee assignments, advancement opportunities, and internal discipline, it reinforces itself across election cycles and administrations.

Think Tanks: Factories of Manufactured Consent

But influence does not only operate through money or career advancement. It also operates through ideas—and this is where think tanks play their part.

Think tanks present themselves as nonpartisan or independent research institutions. In reality, many function as ideological laundromats—funded by billionaires, corporations, and partisan interests to give academic polish to predetermined outcomes.

Their model is simple:

- Wealthy donors fund "research" projects aligned with their ideological agenda
- Policy analysts and scholars are recruited who share these views
- Reports are produced that justify donor-preferred policies
- Lawmakers cite these reports to justify legislation
- Media outlets repeat the findings as neutral expertise

In short, think tanks launder elite interests into the bloodstream of public policy. Their influence is subtle but pervasive—shaping debates before the public even knows they're happening.

A recommendation to slash corporate taxes becomes more palatable when it comes from a "respected institute." A push to dismantle environmental protections gains legitimacy when framed by a "bipartisan policy centre." These ideas do not compete in a marketplace of free thought. They are elevated by design.

Many think tanks operate across party lines. They place former staffers in legislative offices. They advise both Republicans and Democrats. They train the next generation of policy professionals—ensuring ideological continuity masked as intellectual diversity.

But the glue that binds these institutions to real power is, once again, the party system. It is through the centralisation of influence within parties that think tank recommendations become law. The feedback loop is closed: donors fund the research, the research informs the party platform, the party enforces the agenda, and the lobbyists implement the policy.

Brody Mullins lays bare this disturbing reality: behind nearly every major piece of federal legislation lies a complex network of corporate lawyers, policy consultants, and industry insiders who draft, revise, and negotiate the very language of the bills. Elected officials serve as figureheads—the names on the legislation, not its authors.

The process is efficient. It's also invisible.

- **Corporate lobbyists present pre-written bill text to lawmakers**
- **That text is inserted into larger omnibus bills, often unread by most members**
- **Amendments are negotiated in private—not through public deliberation, but through private deals**
- **Party whips enforce discipline, ensuring the final bill is passed without meaningful debate**

To see this system in action, look no further than two of the most consequential laws of the last two decades: the Affordable Care Act (ACA) and the 2017 Tax Cuts and Jobs Act.

The ACA was publicly framed as a moral crusade to expand healthcare access. But behind closed doors, lobbyists from the pharmaceutical and insurance industries were already writing the script. The public option—a government-run insurance alternative—was eliminated early in negotiations. Price controls on prescription drugs were removed. Individual mandates were inserted to guarantee new customers for private insurers.

These weren't compromises. They were conditions—set by corporate actors who had a seat at the table before the public even knew there was a table.

The 2017 Tax Cuts and Jobs Act followed the same playbook. While sold as a middle-class tax cut, it was shaped by corporate lobbyists who wrote provisions benefiting their clients:

- **Pass-through loopholes tailored for hedge funds and real estate**
- **A repatriation holiday on offshore profits**
- **Temporary tax breaks for individuals, but permanent ones for corporations**

Modern lobbying, as Mullins documents, is no longer about persuasion. It's about *placement*. Influence is no longer the art of convincing—it is the science of insertion. Insert language into bills. Insert staffers into committees. Insert lobbyists into strategy meetings. And at the core of this efficiency lies the political party system.

Political parties reduce the complex, messy business of democracy into a series of predictable, controllable checkpoints. For those seeking to influence government—especially those with the money to do it—this centralisation is a gift.

Rather than courting a diverse, decentralised group of independently minded representatives, lobbyists can focus their resources on a handful of critical players:

- **Party leaders**
- **Committee chairs**
- **Legislative aides**

- Think tank insiders
- Campaign managers

Capture these nodes, and the entire system responds.

Party whips ensure members vote the right way. Campaign donations ensure loyalty is rewarded. Media platforms aligned with party messaging keep the public focused on culture war distractions instead of policy betrayal. It's a machine—and it functions precisely because its moving parts are controlled from the top.

This is the central paradox: the very structure that claims to represent the people is designed to *filter them out*. Every layer of party infrastructure exists to manage, constrain, and redirect public will—not amplify it.

In a functioning democracy, political parties would be one of many ways for people to organise. But in the United States, they have become the only viable route to power. Independent candidates face nearly insurmountable obstacles:

- They are excluded from debates
- They receive no party funding
- They lack access to internal polling and strategy
- They are smeared as "spoilers" or "unelectable" by partisan media
- They are deprived of donor networks and institutional endorsements

The two-party system, like a duopoly in the marketplace, exists to eliminate competition. By presenting only two options, both shaped by the same donor class, the system creates the illusion of choice while maintaining elite control. Voters can participate, but they cannot truly disrupt.

The idea that an outsider can rise through this system is technically true—but practically meaningless. Any candidate who challenges party orthodoxy is quickly neutralised. If they gain traction, they are co-opted. If they resist, they are crushed.

At first glance, the system appears democratic. Elections are held. Debates are televised. Candidates campaign and compete. The rituals are real.

But beneath the surface, the machinery tells a different story:

- **Donors select the candidates**
- **Lobbyists draft the legislation**
- **Think tanks justify the policies**
- **Media spin the narrative**
- **Parties enforce compliance**
- **Voters are given the illusion of input**

Political parties are no longer democratic institutions. They are mechanisms of elite preservation. They absorb popular energy and re-channel it into safe, predictable outcomes. They exist not to reflect society, but to discipline it.

This is how democracy is subverted—not through violence, but through systems. Not by cancelling elections, but by predetermining their outcomes. Not by silencing speech, but by ensuring that only certain voices are heard—and only on terms that do not threaten the architecture of control.

This is why both major parties in the U.S. support endless war, corporate bailouts, mass surveillance, and tax cuts for the wealthy—even as they pretend to offer different visions. Because the conflict is a script. The debate is a distraction. And the audience is not meant to intervene.

Voters are asked to choose which flavour of subservience they prefer. And when they reject both options, they are blamed for their own disillusionment—told they are apathetic, ignorant, or radical.

Every few years, a wave of reformers promises to clean up the mess: campaign finance reform, term limits, ethics committees, independent watchdogs. And every time, the structure adapts. Loopholes are exploited. New channels of influence emerge. The cycle continues.

Why? Because the problem is not the players. It is the game.

No amount of regulation can fix a system designed to serve wealth over will. No watchdog can bite when its budget is controlled by the very people it must police. No reform can succeed while power remains centralised in two private organisations that owe nothing to the public—and everything to their funders.

This is why incrementalism fails. It patches the cracks while leaving the foundation untouched.

What's needed is a new architecture—one that decentralises power, dissolves the gatekeeping role of parties, and restores genuine representation through direct accountability.

Chapter 3

Defending the Indefensible

Debunking the Twelve Myths of Party Democracy

In almost every modern democracy, political parties are seen not merely as a feature of governance, but as its essential infrastructure. They are so deeply embedded in the institutional fabric that it becomes difficult to imagine a functioning political system without them. From primary school civics lessons to the highest academic circles, the message is clear: democracy needs parties to operate. This claim, though often unexamined, forms the cornerstone of political orthodoxy in both practice and theory.

Supporters of the party system argue that political parties are a natural and necessary evolution of representative democracy—an efficient means of organising mass participation, streamlining political debate, and delivering coherent governance. These arguments are not just floated by politicians and journalists; they are reinforced by think tanks, professors, donors, and institutions that benefit from maintaining the status quo.

The belief that democracy and parties are inseparable is so deeply entrenched that it is rarely questioned—let alone subjected to rigorous challenge.

While parties were never written into the original blueprints of democracy—and in some cases were explicitly warned against—they have inserted themselves as gatekeepers of the entire system.

And in doing so, they have transformed the meaning and functioning of democracy itself.

Historically, political parties emerged not as philosophical necessities, but as practical tools in the fight for power. They were born out of conflict—ideological, regional, and economic. Parties helped organise groups with shared interests, allowing them to compete more effectively in legislative arenas. But what began as a method of cooperation quickly evolved into machinery of control. As political competition intensified, so too did the desire to centralise decision-making, control nominations, enforce voting discipline, and dominate narratives. The party became not just a vehicle for representation, but a structure designed to capture and wield power.

Over time, the party system became institutionalised. Electoral laws began to favour party organisation. Media coverage began to frame politics exclusively through party competition. Public funding, parliamentary rules, and even candidate eligibility requirements were all built around the assumption that parties were not only necessary but beneficial. In some countries, candidates without party affiliation are seen as fringe by default—regardless of their ideas, competence, or public support.

And so, a self-reinforcing loop emerged. Parties dominated politics, so the system rewarded party behaviour. The system rewarded party behaviour, so more politicians behaved like party loyalists. The more entrenched the system became, the harder it became to imagine alternatives. What started as a workaround became gospel.

Today, defenders of this system often present their arguments as neutral observations of human nature or political logic. But these arguments are not impartial—they are ideological. They reflect the interests of those who benefit from a structure that limits competition, reduces accountability, and channels all political expression through pre-approved frameworks.

Before addressing the arguments put forward by defenders of the party system, we must first outline what a No-Party democratic model actually looks like. Only then can we expose the central illusion: that political parties are not the natural foundation of democracy, but a deeply flawed construct sold to us as indispensable—when in reality, they are anything but.

Imagine a legislature with no party labels. Where candidates rise through public trust, not backroom endorsements. Where votes are won on merit, not tribal loyalty. And where elected representatives owe allegiance only to the people who chose them—not to a party hierarchy. This isn't a distant ideal. It is the foundation of a No-Party democracy—a system designed not to reform party politics, but to replace it.

At its core, this model restores the true meaning of representation.

In any serious setting—a lawyer defending a client, a diplomat negotiating peace, a union leader advocating for workers—representation means acting in the direct interest of those one serves.

Party-based politics inverts this principle. Elected officials are expected to serve the party first, not the people.

Power is concentrated at the top, while representatives are reduced to obedient middlemen.

A No-Party model breaks that distortion.

Candidates stand as individuals, not faction operatives. There are no party whips, no central manifestos, no backroom deals dictating how members vote. Each representative is accountable to their constituents alone, free to act in the public interest—just as true representatives should.

Any eligible citizen can put themselves forward to become a representative. To qualify for the ballot, they must gather a required number of signatures from constituents, demonstrating genuine grassroots support. Candidates are selected based on their individual merits, qualifications, reputations, and policy platforms—with no reference to political parties. All candidates who meet the nomination threshold receive equal public funding to engage with voters, and may also accept additional support from any group or faction, provided all contributions are transparently declared on the ballot paper. Each candidate's top ten priorities are displayed alongside a breakdown of campaign donations by source, promoting accountability and informed choice.

They are backed by a diverse range of supporters—reflecting the complexity of the constituency they serve.

Leadership, too, is selected through a merit-based, transparent process.

There are no party primaries, media coronations, or elite pre-selections. Instead, once the independent legislature is formed, any elected representative may nominate themselves or another for national leadership.

This No-Party model is designed to adapt to both parliamentary and presidential systems. In countries like the UK, where executive leadership is traditionally drawn from within the legislature, candidates for Prime Minister and Shadow Prime Minister would be nominated from among the elected representatives. By contrast, in presidential systems such as the United States, where the President is not selected from the legislature, the model allows for broader nominations—including qualified individuals from outside the chamber. In both cases, the process remains grounded in transparency and merit: nominations arise through open deliberation among independent representatives, and the final two candidates are presented to the public for a national vote.

These final two candidates are then presented to the public in a general election.

The winner becomes head of government; the runner-up becomes the official leader of the opposition. Both roles are therefore publicly mandated, ensuring legitimacy for both governance and scrutiny.

This structure preserves the necessary balance between executive power and democratic accountability—without relying on party machinery to provide it. This candidate-centred model sharply contrasts with today's party-dominated reality.

Without party branding, voters must assess candidates based on their ideas, integrity, and record. Once elected, representatives form coalitions on an issue-by-issue basis. Sovereignty is restored—not just in theory, but in practice—through each independently elected representative.

This model answers the warnings of democratic thinkers across centuries. Aristotle feared factionalism would destabilise the polis. Rousseau warned it would corrupt the general will. The American Founding Fathers called parties "potent engines" of division.

What modern democracies now call political parties are precisely what these thinkers feared: permanent factions, legitimised under the banner of freedom, yet hostile to its substance.

A No-Party democracy does not eliminate interest groups—it simply refuses to hand any of them the machinery of the state.

Unions, student movements, faith communities, businesses—all may endorse candidates. But no group holds guaranteed power.

This decentralised, representative-led system stands in stark contrast to today's reality, where ruling elite factions capture institutions to entrench their power. They fund campaigns, rig leadership contests, and populate party structures with loyal operatives. Independent voices are filtered out; obedient servants are promoted.

A No-Party system doesn't silence these actors—it denies them control. With no party structure to capture, even the wealthiest factions must compete openly for each seat.

The result is honest representation. A parliament or a congress becomes a mirror of the people, not just the parties. Consensus is built through dialogue, not dictated by party leadership. Legitimacy flows not from branding or partisanship, but from trust earned through open, representative governance.

In summary, the No-Party system offers:

- **Independent candidates elected without party logos or central approval**
- **Accountability to voters, not party bosses**
- **Freedom of conscience, with no whip-enforced voting**
- **Governance based on deliberation, not obedience**
- **Resistance to elite capture by removing structural gateways to power**

This is no thought experiment or political theory. This is democracy—freed from the cage of party loyalty.

With the No-Party alternative now outlined, we turn to the defenders of the party system—and ask whether their arguments withstand serious scrutiny.

1. *The Efficiency Illusion—How Parties Centralise, Not Coordinate*

The most common argument in favour of political parties is that they provide a structured framework for governance. By grouping like-minded individuals under a shared platform, parties are said to simplify legislation, form stable majorities, and reduce chaos in complex societies. They sort representatives into ideological blocs, supposedly transforming a multitude of voices into a coherent legislature.

But this rests on a flawed assumption: that the only path to coordination is through rigid, top-down party structures. In reality, parties do not eliminate chaos. They centralise it. What appears as "efficiency" often conceals the suppression of individual judgment, local accountability, and open debate. A No-Party system offers a more democratic alternative, enabling coordination without coercion, and order without conformity.

In both parliamentary and presidential systems, effective governance already hinges not on parties, but on executive leadership through cabinets. The prime minister or president appoints ministers or secretaries to lead departments and implement the administration's agenda. In parliamentary systems like UK, ministers are usually drawn from the legislature and can introduce legislation; in presidential systems like USA, they are external appointees, while Congress drives the legislative process.

Crucially, a No-Party model retains this executive structure but strengthens public oversight. It includes both a governing leadership and a formal opposition: a prime minister or president with their cabinet, and a shadow counterpart with their own team, each publicly mandated and publicly financed. This parallel structure ensures policy direction and scrutiny, offering transparency and accountability. Importantly, the opposition reflects alternative public mandates, not internal party rivalry.

In current party-based systems, real power typically rests with executive leadership, while ordinary legislators are expected to follow the party line, enforced through whips. In contrast, a No-Party legislature enables representatives to vote freely, guided by the interests of their constituents and the substance of each proposal. Leadership remains, but without coercive discipline, creating space for genuine deliberation and independent judgment.

Defenders of party systems often argue that, without partisan organisation, legislatures would fragment into chaos. But this assumes no alternative structure exists to ensure coherence. In reality, the No-Party model provides exactly that: a structured system with a clear executive and opposition, both selected through transparent processes and backed by democratic mandates.

Coordination under this model arises naturally-through issue-based coalitions, legislative committees, and regional alliances. Representatives can collaborate on specific policy areas such as health, education, defence, or the environment, forming practical, purpose-driven partnerships. This already happens within many committees, where cross-party cooperation often produces more effective legislation than rigid, party-driven agendas.

Party advocates also claim that only political parties can aggregate diverse interests into long-term programs, helping voters make informed choices and ensuring accountability. But this coherence is more myth than reality. In the United States, for example, successive presidents from the same party—Clinton, Obama, Biden—have advanced markedly different agendas.

Worse still, in systems without term limits dominant party leaders can remain in or near power for decades, suppressing renewal and dissent under the guise of legitimacy. Far from aggregating interests in a democratic way, such systems often entrench elites and erode accountability.

A No-Party model avoids these contradictions while still offering voters clarity and choice. National candidates—narrowed through deliberation by elected representatives and chosen by public vote—present distinct policy visions on key issues like taxation, welfare, environmental protection, military intervention, and financial regulation.

Meanwhile, local representatives are not bound to a party brand. They run on personal priorities, and voters can assess them based on integrity, performance, and policy. This dual clarity—principled national leadership and independent local accountability—is what parties claim to offer, but is more reliably delivered in a No-Party system.

Supporters of party systems argue that shared platforms provide continuity and enable long-term planning. However, party platforms are often vague, flexible, and easily abandoned once in office. Campaign promises and public interest are frequently overridden by lobbyists, donors, or internal party factions.

In contrast, No-Party governance can offer even greater continuity. Elections still present voters with distinct national visions, but the difference lies in how those visions are implemented and held accountable. In a No-Party model, leaders with clear mandates must work alongside independent legislators who are not bound by party loyalty. If a leader's policies diverge from their promises, these legislators are free to vote them down.

Additionally, voters in a No-Party system have a clearer understanding of what their local candidates stand for. Since candidates run on their own platforms—rather than vague or shifting party lines—constituents can assess them based on specific promises made during the campaign. Unlike party manifestos, which often blur personal responsibility, No-Party campaigns make accountability direct and personal.

Ironically, the dysfunction often blamed on fragmented legislatures is more often the result of party politics. In the U.S., shutdowns and gridlock arise from two entrenched blocs refusing to cooperate for strategic advantage. In the UK, MPs are routinely forced to vote against local interests to satisfy party leadership. And in fragile coalition governments, no single party holds real authority, while opposition becomes too scattered to provide effective scrutiny. In such systems, governance is frequently reduced to deal-making, not principled leadership, leaving urgent issues unresolved and voters disillusioned.

In a No-Party system, representatives are free to cooperate across lines without fear of punishment. This fosters more constructive and responsive governance.

2. *The Illusion of Choice—How Parties Confuse More Than They Clarify*

Another major claim is that political parties clarify the electoral process by offering voters coherent, recognisable choices. Rather than evaluating individual candidates on a case-by-case basis, voters are invited to align themselves with broader ideological identities—left, right, centre, progressive, conservative, nationalist, etc. Parties thus simplify political decision-making and give elections a narrative structure: voters aren't choosing between hundreds of personalities, but between competing visions of the nation's future.

At first glance, political parties seem to offer a convenient framework: broad ideological camps that distil complex policy debates into digestible choices. Left versus right. Progressive versus conservative. But this perceived clarity is, in reality, a false simplicity, a narrative structure that replaces substance with spectacle, and authentic representation with unthinking allegiance.

Party loyalty masks ideological volatility. A change in leadership can drastically shift a party's direction, while the label remains the same-creating the illusion of continuity where none exists. Consider the UK Labour Party: under Jeremy Corbyn, it moved sharply to the left, only to swing back to the centre-right under Keir Starmer. Before both, Tony Blair rebranded it as "New Labour," with pro-market, centrist policies. Yet throughout, the party name never changed.

Some defenders of party systems try to resolve this inconsistency by calling for more parties, not fewer-arguing that a wider range of parties would better represent a wider range of views. But this approach comes with its own trade-offs. In systems with many parties, ideological lines often blur, and the sheer number of options can overwhelm rather than empower voters. In countries like Germany, the Netherlands, or France, voters often struggle to distinguish not just between similarly named parties, but between parties offering nearly identical platforms. The multiplication of labels rarely brings greater clarity. Instead, party branding adds another layer of confusion.

Worse still, multi-party systems often lead to unstable coalitions. Parties are forced to compromise-not just with allies, but sometimes with ideological opponents-simply to form a government. Promises get diluted, accountability is muddied, and power becomes difficult to trace. When several parties share responsibility, it becomes unclear who is really in charge. The result? Weak governments, weaker opposition, and a public that loses confidence in both.

It's true that many voters rely on shortcuts: party labels, influencers, peer networks, or instinct. But this reality should not be used to justify the dominance of party machines. Instead, we should ask: Why do so many voters feel disengaged or under-informed in the first place? And who benefits from that disengagement?

The answer, at least in part, lies with the very system defenders seek to preserve. Modern party politics encourages passivity. It reduces complex debates to binary slogans. It conditions voters to respond to branding, not substance, to vote by tribe rather than by merit.

A No-Party system doesn't expect voters to become policy experts. It simply removes the structural barriers that obstruct better engagement. Candidates must still earn trust and attention, and image will always play a role-but the signals voters respond to would emerge from the candidates themselves, not from a centralised party machine. Clarity would still exist: presidential or prime ministerial candidates could present broad, recognisable positions. Some voters might study manifestos; others might rely on lived experience, community reputation, or past performance.

In most party democracies, labels often obscure more than they clarify. Voters are routinely presented with a false choice between parties that share financial backers, embrace similar economic models, and support the same foreign policy frameworks, despite appearing ideologically opposed. In the U.S., both major parties are heavily funded by corporate interests, Wall Street, and the military-industrial complex.

Even ideological branding offers no guarantee of consistency. Centre-left parties that once stood for workers' rights have implemented austerity and privatisation. Centre-right parties promising fiscal discipline have inflated deficits through corporate bailouts. Increasingly, party identity is about marketing, not principle, shaped by pollsters and consultants, not values.

Contrast this with a No-Party system, where candidates are elected individually by their local constituencies, each campaigning on a clearly stated platform tailored to their community's needs. In local elections, voters would select the candidate they trust most, based on their stance on specific, tangible issues. In general elections, where a head of government is chosen, voters would naturally shift focus to broader ideological questions.

Ironically, many people already vote based on broad value alignment, not detailed party manifestos. Yet defenders of the party system make a contradictory claim: they argue that voters don't understand policy detail, while simultaneously insisting that parties are vital because they represent clear policy positions. A No-Party system doesn't expect voters to become technocrats, but it does reveal the hollowness of party branding and respects the electorate's ability to judge candidates on clarity, integrity, and relevance.

Far from overwhelming the electorate, removing party branding can foster deeper engagement. Without tribal labels, candidates must earn support through transparency, accessibility, and ideas, not inherited identity. And at the local level, where choices are limited and stakes are tangible, voters are well placed to make informed decisions without reverting to crude ideological shorthand.

The belief that parties offer "competing national visions" is increasingly a myth. Those visions are often manufactured—by donors, think tanks, and PR firms. A No-Party system reclaims that vision for the people, by empowering independent representatives who reflect the actual diversity of public thought. Even within a No-Party model, competing national visions can still emerge, through presidential campaigns, policy debates, and ideological positioning. But they do so organically.

Crucially, the kind of narrative clarity that parties claim to offer comes at a steep cost: polarisation. Party identity hardens divisions and transforms politics into tribal warfare. Voters stop debating ideas and start defending sides. While some loyalty or identity-based politics is inevitable, there's a fundamental difference between organic alignment and the institutionalised division enforced by parties.

No-Party governance doesn't eliminate political loyalty, but it removes the scaffolding that institutionalises it: centralised messaging, lifelong labels, and party-aligned media machines. It allows political identity to become more local, more flexible, and more rooted in actual issues, making room for disagreement without turning every debate into a zero-sum battle.

3. *The Accountability Mirage—How Parties Shield, Not Expose, Political Failure*

Proponents claim that political parties enhance accountability by creating identifiable units of responsibility. If a government performs poorly, voters can punish the entire party at the next election. This mechanism, they argue, promotes discipline and coherence, making it easier to judge performance and outcomes. A failed policy, a broken promise, or a scandal doesn't get lost in a sea of individuals—it becomes attached to the party brand, and the electorate can respond accordingly.

But this argument quickly unravels under scrutiny.

First, it conflates brand recognition with actual accountability. What it offers is the illusion of recourse, not meaningful consequences. When voters are given only two or three parties to choose from—each often funded by the same donors, advised by the same consultants, and shaped by the same elite consensus—punishing one party simply hands power to another that functions in nearly identical ways. The rotation of power between parties becomes ritualistic rather than transformative. Policy trajectories remain largely unchanged.

Consider war, austerity, deregulation, surveillance, or corporate bailouts. In country after country, whether centre-left or centre-right is in power, these policies continue with minimal deviation. When the consequences arrive—economic collapse, social unrest, eroded public services—no single individual or institution is held to account. Parties scapegoat each other, blame circumstances, or claim insufficient mandate.

More disturbingly, party-based accountability encourages collective punishment rather than individual responsibility. A corrupt or incompetent minister can hide behind the party banner, shielded by loyalty and protected by the party machine. Voters may want to punish that individual, but they're forced to cast a vote for or against the entire party. This dynamic protects insiders and silences dissenters within the party's own ranks, creating a culture of conformity.

A No-Party system enhances accountability by removing this veil. Each elected representative stands on their own record. If a lawmaker fails to deliver on promises, votes in ways inconsistent with their stated values, or becomes embroiled in scandal, they can be held directly accountable by their constituents—without punishing unrelated representatives who have served with integrity.

Moreover, the idea that voters can "punish a party" presumes a level of coherence within that party that rarely exists. Parties are often broad tents, encompassing factions with deeply contradictory policies. One wing may favour military intervention; another opposes it. One bloc may champion environmental reform; another quietly blocks it. So when a party is punished, which faction within it is being rejected?

And finally, party loyalty often masks accountability rather than enabling it. In a whip-driven system, even well-intentioned representatives are compelled to vote in line with party leadership. The result is not principled governance, but manufactured consensus. When unpopular or harmful policies are passed, voters cannot tell who truly supported them and who voted under duress.

In a No-Party system, such distortion is much harder. Representatives are free to act according to their conscience and the mandate of their constituents. Their votes, their actions, and their statements stand on their own.

In short, the promise of party accountability is a mirage. It centralises blame without delivering justice, obscures who is responsible for what, and suppresses the very mechanisms through which voters can meaningfully judge their representatives. True accountability comes from empowering citizens to elect individuals they can scrutinise, challenge, and replace.

4. *The Stability Myth—How Parties Manufacture Order and Suppress Dissent*

One of the most enduring justifications for political parties is the claim that they promote stability. By bundling ideas, managing dissent internally, and organising both government and opposition, parties are said to create a predictable framework for governance. They prevent chaos, we are told, by giving voters and lawmakers a clear structure, thereby reducing volatility and insulating society from factional breakdown or civil conflict.

But beneath this polished logic lies a more unsettling reality.

Party systems do not eliminate factionalism—they merely disguise it. Internal party divisions are often every bit as sharp as those between parties themselves. In many cases, the fiercest disagreements are not between opposing parties, but between factions within them. The only difference is that these divisions are suppressed, contained, and hidden from public view in the name of "unity." Rather than fostering stability, this enforced coherence breeds resentment, stifles open debate, and leads to a politics of managed illusion.

Indeed, the kind of "stability" produced by party politics is not the calm of consensus but the stagnation of closed systems. When real dissent is managed through spin doctors and party whips, rather than aired openly in the public square, political energy doesn't disappear—it festers. Parties suppress the visible symptoms of instability, but they rarely address the root causes. Public frustration, disillusionment, and alienation grow under the surface, waiting for a breaking point.

We can see this in countries like the United States, where the two-party system has not prevented polarisation but has instead exacerbated it. The appearance of stability—guaranteed by the predictable alternation of power between Democrats and Republicans—conceals a deep rot: record-low trust in institutions, legislative gridlock, and rising extremism on both ends of the spectrum. Similarly, in the UK, the Labour–Conservative duopoly has ensured continuity of power, not continuity of good governance.

Proponents of party systems often raise the spectre of chaos in non-party systems—pointing to unstable coalition governments or legislative deadlock. But these examples confuse messiness with dysfunction. A political system that allows real, open disagreement is not inherently unstable; it is dynamic. Conflict, when transparent and accountable, is not a threat to democracy—it is democracy in action.

Under the No-Party model, representatives are not shackled by party directives. Instead, they must negotiate, build consensus, and form working coalitions on each issue. This demands more deliberation, yes—but it also builds more legitimacy. It discourages ideological rigidity and fosters pragmatic solutions based on the real needs of constituents.

5. Structure Without Submission: Structuring Governance and Opposition in a No-Party System

One of the most frequently cited virtues of political parties is the stability they allegedly bring to governance. Proponents argue that without coherent party blocs, democracies risk descending into disarray—plagued by gridlock, fragmented representation, and short-lived coalitions. This view is particularly common in critiques of proportional representation systems, where parliaments are often composed of multiple small parties forming unstable governing alliances. In such systems, critics point to opportunistic coalition-building and endless compromise as evidence that democracy without strong party structures is inherently flawed.

However, it would be a mistake to conflate the weaknesses of multi-party coalition governments with the No-Party representative model proposed here. This is not a referendum-based system where ordinary citizens vote on legislation directly, nor does it rely on public opinion to determine day-to-day policy. Instead, it preserves representative democracy—but without the distortions of party control.

In place of party bargaining or ideological blocs, the No-Party system delivers coherent governance through a nationally mandated executive—including a directly elected President or Prime Minister, and a parallel Shadow President or Shadow Prime Minister. These roles are not defined by party allegiance, but by merit, transparency, and broad support from within the chamber of independently elected representatives—individuals who are expected to engage seriously with legislation, policy, and the national interest. One can argue that this will end up being like two party system government and opposition splitting the legislature. This is partially correct that yes there will be government and opposition but these will have to argue for or against any proposed legislation.

Accountability in this model is grounded in clear, issue-specific votes by these representatives. Each elected official is accountable to their constituency. Legislative coherence emerges from the democratic alignment of individual representatives around shared national priorities, with the freedom to vote on each issue according to their mandate and informed judgment.

6. The Loyalty Machine—Why Party Systems Suppress Leadership

Political parties are often praised as institutions that train and vet future leaders. From local organisers and party volunteers to MPs, senators, and cabinet ministers, the party system is said to offer a clear path for civic engagement and political development. The idea is that long-term involvement in a party exposes individuals to the inner workings of government and policymaking, preparing them for higher office in a system that rewards merit and commitment.

Defenders of political parties often argue that parties are essential for nurturing leadership. They present the party structure as a ladder—where ambitious, civic-minded individuals can start at the grassroots, learn the ropes of public service, and ascend through the ranks based on merit, experience, and commitment. This pathway, we are told, produces better leaders and ensures a steady supply of individuals prepared to govern.

In theory, this sounds admirable. In practice, however, it is largely a myth. What parties cultivate above all else is loyalty—not leadership. The supposed training process is less about learning how to serve the public, and more about learning how to serve the party. Aspiring politicians quickly realise that advancement is not primarily based on ideas, integrity, or competence, but on allegiance to the party hierarchy.

Far from being a school of democratic leadership, the party system often resembles a patronage network. It filters out independence, critical thinking, and innovation—the very qualities needed in a functioning democracy. This isn't just a theoretical concern; it's observable in almost every party-dominated system. Candidates are parachuted into constituencies they have no connection to. Debate is stifled by the party whip. Talented local figures are passed over because they don't "fit the brand." And the few who dare to dissent—even from within—are pushed to the margins.

Consider the countless young activists and campaigners who enter party politics with genuine ideals, only to find their principles diluted or abandoned in the pursuit of advancement. Many learn quickly that toeing the line is the only route to influence. Others leave disillusioned. Party loyalty becomes the currency of political survival, and career politicians rise not by challenging power, but by mastering its language.

This dynamic is not unique to one country or one ideology. It is built into the very structure of party politics. Even where primaries exist, as in the United States, those backed by party machines and big donors are far more likely to succeed. The training, such as it is, is in how to fundraise, how to deflect scrutiny, and how to stay "on message".

In No-Party systems, any citizen with community respect, expertise, or a compelling vision can put themselves forward. They rise based on public trust. Their "training" comes from real-world experience—running a school, a hospital, a business, a community organisation—and from being directly answerable to voters.

True leadership is tested in service, not in obedience. And true public servants don't need to be groomed within a political brand to understand what justice, fairness, or accountability look like. In fact, many of the most principled and effective political figures in modern history—from whistleblowers and activists to community organisers and independent reformers—began outside the party system, not within it.

7. *The Unity Illusion—How Parties Silence Diversity in the Name of Cohesion*

Political parties are often presented as unifying forces in pluralistic societies. By assembling broad coalitions—students and unions, farmers and manufacturers, minorities and business elites—they claim to foster dialogue, temper extremism, and provide a framework for national cohesion.

Yet this unity comes at a cost.

Rather than authentically representing diverse voices, party coalitions are primarily designed to consolidate power. To maintain internal harmony, contradictions are glossed over, dissenting voices silenced, and minority interests marginalized. Communities that don't align neatly with the dominant narrative are reduced to vote banks: courted during elections, but excluded from meaningful influence once power is secured.

Advocates argue that broad coalitions moderate extremism by absorbing radical elements. But this assumption is increasingly shaky. In practice, parties often stoke division to energize their base—adopting extreme rhetoric, co-opting fringe ideas, and portraying compromise as weakness.

By contrast, a No-Party system allows for unity without suppressing diversity. In such a model, the two final candidates in a general election must appeal to a wide cross-section of voters, transcending social, economic, and cultural divides. Without inherited platforms or rigid ideologies, candidates are compelled to engage directly with varied communities and craft inclusive messages that reflect real public priorities.

In a No-Party framework, ideological diversity is expressed through free alignment. While party systems can evolve-sometimes drastically, these shifts usually hinge on the personal influence of individual figures rather than structural openness. Voters don't just support parties; they place enormous weight on leaders. That's why, in systems like the UK, party leaders often resign after electoral defeat; and in countries like the U.S., leadership changes can dramatically reshape party platforms. Yet even then, candidates remain tethered to the constraints of party identity and tradition.

In a No-Party system, candidates present themselves-and their policies-directly to the public. They are not bound by party orthodoxy. One election might feature two candidates advocating lower taxes; the next could present a choice between higher public spending and fiscal conservatism. The point is not party loyalty, but policy choice. Voters support individuals who reflect their values, and those individuals are accountable to the people.

In the party system, many groups are strategically contained rather than empowered. Party leaders, aware that certain communities—such as ethnic or religious minorities—are unlikely to support openly nationalist or populist parties, often take them for granted. These voters are courted with symbolic gestures and vague promises, then sidelined post-election.

A striking example emerged in the 2024 U.S. election. Despite Donald Trump's earlier travel ban targeting Muslim-majority countries, some Muslim leaders shifted support toward him-not out of ideological alignment, but in protest. Frustrated by President Biden's inaction on the war in Gaza, they viewed Trump's promises to "stop wars" as a strategic, if desperate, alternative. It wasn't an endorsement of his platform, but a rebuke of the Democratic Party's failure to engage.

Within parties, unity is rarely democratic. Internal compromise happens in backrooms, brokered by elites and donors-not through grassroots debate. This is not unity, but uniformity by suppression.

No-Party systems offer a more empowering alternative. When candidates stand on individual platforms in local, issue-based elections, communities can form their own coalitions. Ethnic, religious, and ideological groups can back candidates who truly reflect their values, forging alliances transparently.

In truth, party systems generate polarisation. As parties strive to hold coalitions together, they define themselves by opposition—manufacturing enemies, caricaturing dissenters, and fostering tribal loyalty. The "broad tent" becomes a battleground of conflicting agendas, held together by branding and expediency.

If national unity is the goal, it won't come from squeezing everyone under two or three umbrellas. It will emerge from empowering communities to voice their priorities freely and elect representatives who are accountable to them.

8. The Consistency Trap—Why Party Ideology Sacrifices Public Interest

One of the most persistent claims made in defence of political parties is that they promote ideological coherence and consistency in government. A party that wins power, it is said, carries a clear manifesto and a unified ideological vision, enabling smoother policymaking and the implementation of long-term reforms. By grouping like-minded individuals, parties are thought to reduce internal contradictions and prevent legislative gridlock.

But this defence only considers one alternative to party politics: a system of disconnected, independent representatives. In contrast, the proposed No-Party model also offers coherent policy platforms, often with greater clarity, transparency, and accountability. Under this model, both presidential or prime ministerial candidates would publish detailed public manifestos during their campaigns. These would be comprehensive governing plans that include:

- **Legislative priorities**
- **Economic and social policies**
- **Governance philosophy**
- **Key national objectives**

When voters go to the polls in this system, they are not simply choosing between personalities or blindly backing a party brand. Instead, they make an informed choice between two leadership teams, each led by a candidate and their chosen running mate and guided by a clear, published programme. And because there is no party machinery to deflect blame or spin failure, both governing and opposition leaders remain directly visible and accountable for their promises, performance, and integrity.

As for the claim that parties offer long-term consistency, the evidence suggests otherwise. Party-led governments frequently shift direction with changes in leadership. Party ideology is rarely stable beyond a single electoral cycle. Tony Blair's Labour Party bore little resemblance to its earlier form-just as the Democratic Party under Joe Biden differs significantly from the one led by Barack Obama, or by Bill Clinton before him. Rather than guaranteeing stability, party politics often delivers rebranding, contradictions, and policy reversals.

Perhaps the more decisive difference lies not in what leaders promise, but in how they rise to power. In traditional party systems, political leaders must climb a ladder built by elite interests. By the time they reach the top, they are entangled in obligations-to financiers, internal factions, and powerful groups with expectations of influence.

In contrast, No-Party candidates—both for government and shadow leadership—are selected through transparent, independent processes and are accountable only to the public. Their authority derives solely from popular support, and they carry no debt to those who traditionally buy access to power. This independence forms the foundation of a democratic system where policy is shaped by public interest, not private influence.

Of course, no system is entirely immune to elite interference. Even in a No-Party democracy, wealthy donors may attempt to bankroll candidates in the final stages of a campaign. But their influence is structurally limited, not just by transparency, but by the design of the system itself.

First, No-Party candidates are not chosen through donor-funded primaries or internal party deals. They are filtered through a broad base of independently elected representatives, who narrow the field to two final contenders based on merit, public service, and integrity. Because their support must come from a wide and diverse group, the final candidates are more likely to hold balanced, broadly acceptable positions.

Second, there is no party apparatus to enforce loyalty or deliver favours. A billionaire might support a candidate, but cannot rely on that candidate—or on any coordinated bloc in parliament—to advance a private agenda. Each representative votes independently. This makes it far harder for wealth to distort policy outcomes.

While parties claim to reduce contradictions and prevent gridlock, the reality is that they often suppress genuine disagreement through coercion. When Boris Johnson expelled 21 Conservative MPs for opposing his Brexit deal, it wasn't to resolve contradictions. It was to enforce obedience. In the U.S., constant infighting within both major parties shows that so-called unity is often a façade maintained by pressure, not principle.

In a No-Party democracy, disagreement is a reflection of a pluralistic society. Without rigid party platforms, voters choose between two independently crafted policy agendas and select the one that best aligns with their priorities. As a result, the winning platform is more likely to reflect the public will. When the public supports a policy, a majority of their independently elected representatives are likely to support it too.

Of course, some representatives may still be self-interested or influenced by donors. No system is immune to corruption. But without party structures to shield them, these individuals are fully exposed to public scrutiny-and far more likely to be replaced at the next election if they break their pledges or act against the public interest. In that sense, the system is self-correcting.

The result is not disorder, but a form of governance where public opinion is more accurately and directly translated into legislation. That's not chaos. That's democracy working as it should.

9. *The Freedom Fallacy—Why Parties Do Not Embody Political Liberty*

At the most philosophical level, some defenders argue that the formation of political parties is itself a democratic right—an expression of freedom of association. If citizens wish to group together to advance common interests, they should be free to do so. Banning or discouraging parties, they claim, would be an authoritarian impulse, one that could suppress political diversity and lead to centralised control. This view casts parties not as threats to democracy, but as the purest expression of it.

The argument that parties are a natural outgrowth of freedom of association is often presented as the philosophical trump card: that people should be free to organise, campaign, and promote ideas collectively. And in principle, this is entirely correct. Freedom of association is fundamental to any democratic society. But to confuse the right to form groups with the institutional entrenchment of political parties in the electoral system is a category error.

People may indeed come together to advocate for shared beliefs, and under a No-Party democracy, they would remain free to form unions, movements, interest groups, or local alliances. What is being challenged is not the freedom to associate or speak—but the idea that such associations should dominate ballot papers, control candidate selection, and monopolise legislative power. When parties are the only viable route to office, the freedom of association becomes reversed: individuals must associate with a party or face near-total exclusion from the political process.

Moreover, political parties today are not spontaneous grassroots associations. They are highly centralised, hierarchically controlled institutions that filter out dissent, enforce rigid loyalty, and often act as vehicles for elite interests. Far from protecting diversity, they reduce political discourse to scripted talking points and binary framing. In many cases, they serve to suppress, not empower, independent thought or minority voices.

True political freedom should mean that citizens can vote for individuals who best represent their local interests, values, and judgment. In a No-Party system, individuals could still campaign on shared values or align with like-minded representatives once in office. Ideological diversity does not disappear in the absence of parties—it is simply expressed more honestly.

To suggest that democracy cannot exist without formal political parties is like saying freedom of religion cannot exist without a state church. Citizens can still form movements, organise collectively, and support causes. The goal of No-Party reform is not to ban association, but to liberate political representation from its capture by institutional factions.

10. The Expertise Argument—Why Parties Don't Hold a Monopoly on Policy Knowledge

One of the more technocratic defences of political parties is that they bring policy expertise and intellectual infrastructure to the democratic process. Party-affiliated think tanks, research departments, media consultants, and policy advisors are said to supply essential knowledge, helping elected officials craft legislation and communicate effectively with the public. The concern is that without this scaffolding, independents would govern in an ad hoc manner, with little coordination or legislative depth.

But this argument assumes—wrongly—that the current party system provides neutral or objective expertise. In practice, party-affiliated policy infrastructure is designed not to pursue the public interest, but to craft and defend the party line. Research is rarely dispassionate; it is filtered through ideological lenses and donor priorities. Communication is not about informing citizens, but about messaging, persuasion, and damage control.

The supposed "expertise" offered by parties also often crowds out independent or locally relevant solutions. Policy priorities are dictated from the top, with little regard for regional variation or constituent-specific concerns. A one-size-fits-all policy platform becomes the standard, and candidates are expected to adopt it wholesale, regardless of whether it aligns with the needs of their district. In this way, expertise becomes centralised, partisan, and detached—a tool to entrench national platforms rather than empower local problem-solving.

In contrast, a No-Party system does not eliminate expertise—it decentralises it. Independent representatives would have access to publicly funded, No-Party research bodies designed to serve all lawmakers, not just those within a party structure. Parliamentary libraries, civil service advisors, academic partnerships, and issue-specific research centres could serve as neutral repositories of knowledge. Rather than channelling all knowledge through party headquarters, expertise would become a shared resource in service of the people—not a weapon for political competition.

Moreover, decentralised governance encourages collaboration between representatives who share concerns, regardless of ideology. In a No-Party assembly, lawmakers concerned with housing, education, healthcare, or defence could voluntarily coordinate, seek input from specialists, and develop legislation with direct feedback from constituents and independent experts.

The current party-based model doesn't enhance expertise—it limits its diversity and application. The idea that democracy would collapse without party messaging teams and spin doctors is less a reflection of what citizens need, and more a defence of the political class's dependence on tightly managed narratives.

Real democracy does not require less expertise—it requires better access to expertise, free from party capture. When policy advice is shaped by the public interest rather than partisan loyalty or donor influence, legislation becomes not just more informed, but more just.

11. *The Faction Fallacy—Why Human Nature Doesn't Justify Party Power*

One of the most fatalistic arguments is that factions—and by extension, parties—are inevitable. As long as human beings have differing interests, values, and priorities, they will form groups. Attempting to build a political system without parties, the argument goes, is fighting against human nature itself. The best we can do is to refine, manage, and regulate these groups through transparent elections and democratic norms.

This argument is often presented as a philosophical dead-end: that factions, and therefore political parties, are simply natural. Wherever human beings gather, there will be disagreement. People form alliances, organise around shared interests, and compete for influence. From families and tribes to religious groups and trade unions, history seems to confirm that humans are social, political, and factional creatures.

This observation is not wrong—but the conclusion often drawn from it is deeply misleading.

Yes, factions are inevitable. What is not inevitable is the formalisation of factions into rigid, centralised, and all-powerful political parties. That is not human nature—it is a specific institutional choice, made in a specific historical context.

Even James Madison, whose Federalist No. 10 is often cited to support this argument, did not advocate institutionalising factions. On the contrary, he warned that factions posed a dangerous threat to the rights of others and to the stability of democratic government. Madison believed that a large and diverse republic could help mitigate the damage done by any one faction dominating the system—not that factions should be given official status, public funding, and the power to control nominations, legislation, and appointments.

The problem is not that people group together—it's that current political systems force those groups into binary or limited-party containers, and then hand those containers the keys to the state. This transforms voluntary civic organisation into compulsory political allegiance. It narrows the range of permissible views, hardens ideological lines, and incentivises conflict over cooperation. Factions become not just expressions of interest—they become the battleground through which all decisions must pass.

In a No-Party system, people are still free to organise—and they will. Not because they're idealists, but precisely because they are human. Self-interest is not abolished; it is channelled. Teachers may back candidates who defend public education. Farmers may organise to protect their livelihoods. Workers, business owners, environmentalists—all can and will form networks driven by their concerns. That's not a flaw in democracy; it's the fuel that drives it. But the critical difference is this: under a No-Party system, these groups can no longer entrench themselves as permanent power blocs. They must compete on ideas—not entitlements. They can influence the debate, but they cannot own the arena. What's removed is not human motivation, but the machinery that turns civic energy into captured institutions. Representation remains rooted in human nature—but it no longer allows that nature to be monopolised by party brands.

No-Party systems do not suppress factions—they simply refuse to grant them privileged status. Citizens can still organise, advocate, and build coalitions. But they must win arguments on the merits, not by default. In a system of independent representatives, interest groups must persuade a majority of lawmakers, not merely capture one party and bulldoze the rest.

This actually encourages more nuanced and issue-specific collaboration. Representatives are free to align on a particular policy—climate change, infrastructure, education—without having to agree on an entire party platform.

Moreover, the idea that party systems are natural ignores the immense resources required to keep them in place: primary systems, central offices, funding pipelines, media arms, disciplinary whips, and donor networks. These are not spontaneous human associations. They are industrial-scale machines, built to control outcomes—not to reflect natural disagreement.

Political diversity is a fact. Party control is a design. We should not confuse the existence of human difference with a justification for entrenching centralised factions in law, in funding, and in the structure of our democracies.

The choice is not between chaos and parties. The choice is whether democracy should be structured around top-down control or bottom-up representation. The inevitability of factions does not require the institutionalisation of party power—it demands that we build systems resilient enough to handle disagreement without turning every election into a zero-sum tribal war.

The arguments used to defend political parties may appear logical on the surface—structure, clarity, accountability, stability, leadership, unity, consistency, freedom, expertise, inevitability. But when held up to scrutiny, each of these pillars begins to crumble.

The No-Party model does not pretend to change human nature. It doesn't seek to erase ambition, loyalty, disagreement, or even tribalism. It simply rewires the system so that those natural tendencies cannot be weaponised. It accepts human nature—and designs around it. This is not a utopian denial of how people behave—it is a system calibrated to ensure that when people do behave selfishly, their influence is checked, visible, and contestable. Reforming democracy doesn't mean reforming the soul.

12. Creating the Monster: How Parties Enable the Extremism They Claim to Prevent

Supporters of the party system often claim that without political parties, democracies would be dangerously vulnerable to populists, demagogues, and extremists. Parties, they argue, serve as essential gatekeepers—filtering out dangerous elements, imposing internal discipline, and preserving institutional norms. This claim, repeated so often it has become dogma, crumbles under even modest historical scrutiny.

In truth, the world's most notorious dictators rose not in the absence of parties, but through them. Political parties were not obstacles to their ascent—they were instruments of it. From Adolf Hitler and Benito Mussolini to Joseph Stalin and Hugo Chávez, authoritarian rulers relied on party structures to manipulate democratic processes, consolidate power, and ultimately dismantle the very institutions they claimed to represent.

Adolf Hitler's rise to power through the Nazi Party is among the most devastating examples. The Nazi Party exploited the weaknesses of the Weimar Republic, using the democratic process to erode democracy itself. Hitler did not seize power in a sudden coup. He was elevated by a party that gained public legitimacy through elections, only to abolish those same democratic mechanisms once in power. Party loyalty—enforced through propaganda, fear, and mass mobilisation—replaced individual accountability. The Nazi regime did not emerge in a vacuum; it was cultivated, funded, and enabled by a party that provided structure, strategy, and ideological coherence.

A similar pattern unfolded in Italy, where Benito Mussolini used the National Fascist Party to channel post-war unrest into a movement of national revival. His infamous March on Rome in 1922 was not a revolution but a calculated use of the party as a tool to gain power legally. Once installed, Mussolini used the party to suppress dissent, crush independent institutions, and impose a corporate authoritarian state. In both cases, the party was not just a means of political expression—it was a weapon of control.

Even in modern mature democracies, parties often do little to contain extremism. Instead, they adapt to it. In the United States, Donald Trump rose to power not outside the Republican Party but through it. After initial resistance, party elites capitulated—supporting his candidacy, adopting his rhetoric, and enabling his attacks on democratic norms. The same dynamic has played out in France, India, and other democracies where party competition encourages leaders to adopt more radical stances to secure their base. Far from filtering out dangerous voices, parties frequently amplify them.

This is no coincidence. The structure of party competition rewards polarisation. It encourages tribalism, inflames cultural divisions, and turns elections into contests of identity and fear. Party leaders are incentivised to energise their base by demonising opponents rather than building consensus. Loyalty, not merit, becomes the path to advancement. As a result, extremists are not filtered out—they are often the most successful players in the game.

As these leaders tighten their grip, the party becomes indistinguishable from the individual. It ceases to function as a representative institution and instead becomes the personal vehicle of the ruler—a tool for control, enrichment, and unchallenged authority. The party is treated like private property, and its internal structures are shaped to serve the whims of one man rather than the will of the people. In such a system, challengers are not debated—they are eliminated. But a No-Party system disrupts this pattern entirely. With no fixed party machinery to inherit or command, there is no party for any one individual to own. Every election resets the political landscape. Power must be earned anew by each candidate, directly from their constituents, without the advantage of inherited branding or institutional loyalty. This continual reset function is a quiet but powerful safeguard against authoritarian consolidation.

No amount of reform can turn a cage into a cradle of liberty.

Chapter 4

The True Price of Loyalty

How Political Parties Fuel War, Division, and National Decline

Behind every war waged without cause, every policy that tears a nation in two, and every crisis that could have been prevented lies a deeper force rarely named: the political party system itself. It is easy to blame ideology, bad leaders, or global events—but those are often symptoms. The root lies in a structure that rewards obedience over wisdom, loyalty over conscience, and division over unity.

Yes, autocracies and empires have launched wars without public consent—but in modern democracies, parties do the same while claiming to represent the people. Once in power, they behave like absolute rulers: ignoring protests, silencing dissent, and pushing through wars the public never endorsed. Parties do not merely respond to conflict—they manufacture it. They turn disagreement into dogma, compromise into betrayal, and public pain into partisan ammunition. And in doing so, they cost us more than money or trust. They cost us lives.

Throughout history, the deadliest wars and most monstrous atrocities did not arise from the will of ordinary people, but from the ambitions of those insulated from accountability. Kings launched crusades. Emperors pursued conquest. Sultans sacrificed millions for imperial glory. In every case, a single ruler—or a cloistered elite—wielded unchecked power, immune to the consequences borne by the masses.

In the 20th century, this dynamic didn't vanish. It evolved.

The crowns of monarchs gave way to party banners. The absolutism of emperors was replaced by presidents and prime ministers, cloaked in democratic legitimacy, yet wielding near-dictatorial authority—especially over war. Whether it was Stalin's purges, Johnson's escalation in Vietnam, or Bush's invasion of Iraq, the common thread was not ideology, but impunity: decisions made without genuine accountability, enabled by party loyalty, institutional machinery, and the suppression of dissent.

Even in so-called free societies, party leaders surround themselves with loyalists, control narratives, and deploy the machinery of state to act with impunity. The illusion of democracy remains intact—but the decisions are still made behind closed doors, insulated from real public consent.

Across history, political parties in so-called democracies have presided over some of the most horrific atrocities of the modern age—not as accidents of policy, but as direct outcomes of party loyalty, imperial ambition, and elite manipulation.

From Vietnam to Iraq, from Algeria to the Congo, millions have died not under dictatorships alone, but under the banners of elected governments. These deaths were not the result of spontaneous chaos, but of structured, bipartisan consensus—often wrapped in the language of democracy, freedom, and national security.

- **In the United States, both Democrats and Republicans escalated wars in Vietnam and Iraq, ignored mass public opposition, and shielded war criminals from accountability.**
- **In Latin America, both parties supported brutal coups, death squads, and military juntas to protect corporate profits and geopolitical control.**

- In Britain, party governments engineered genocidal famines in colonial India and launched illegal invasions like Suez to preserve imperial dominance.
- In France, every major political faction enabled torture, massacres, and internment camps during the Algerian War.
- In Belgium, all parties managed a colonial regime that killed millions in the Congo, continuing its exploitation long after the monarchy's formal rule ended.

Even beyond democratic facades, the party-state structure enabled atrocities on an industrial scale:

- Adolf Hitler's Nazi Party—democratically elected and legally empowered—orchestrated the Holocaust: the systematic extermination of six million Jews, and millions of others deemed undesirable. This was not the work of a lone madman, but a ruling party that legislated hate, mobilised the state, and crushed dissent with fear and propaganda.
- King Leopold II of Belgium, under the guise of personal rule and later party-administered colonialism, oversaw a genocidal regime in the Congo. Millions were enslaved, mutilated, or killed in pursuit of rubber and ivory. Children had their hands cut off for failing to meet quotas. Entire villages were razed to enforce obedience. When Belgian political parties took over, the exploitation continued—cloaked in bureaucracy and respectability.
- Winston Churchill, lionised as a democratic icon, presided over the Bengal Famine of 1943. While millions of Indians starved, Churchill's government prioritised wartime exports and military stockpiling. He blocked relief shipments, mocked the victims,

> and blamed them for "breeding like rabbits." Up to
> 3 million Indians died—not from drought, but from
> deliberate imperial neglect.

These were not historical aberrations. They were the predictable outcomes of concentrated authority filtered through elite-serving party structures.

Even in nations celebrated for their democratic traditions, party politics has repeatedly enabled mass death—not despite democracy, but through its subversion. Parties centralise power, suppress dissent, manipulate consent, and align with elite interests at the expense of human life.

This is the real cost of partisan governance: not just dysfunction or corruption, but millions of corpses, generations of trauma, and entire nations reduced to ruin.

The party system is not a safeguard against atrocity. It is a recurring cause of it.

Since the outbreak of World War I, more than 150 million people have died in wars, genocides, occupations, and interventions—most of them civilians. From the trenches of Europe to the firebombed cities of Asia, from colonial famines to modern drone strikes, the vast majority of these deaths occurred not under rogue regimes, but under the governance of political parties—elected, appointed, or otherwise empowered by systems claiming democratic legitimacy.

The machinery of party rule has enabled two world wars, the atomic bombing of civilians in Hiroshima and Nagasaki, nuclear brinkmanship, and countless interventions marketed as progress. Its cost is not merely dysfunction—it is written in blood and rubble.

Consider the case of Benjamin Netanyahu. Years before the 2003 invasion of Iraq, Netanyahu and his allies were publicly advocating for regime change—not just in Iraq, but in Syria, Libya, Sudan, and Iran. In 2002, he testified before the U.S. Congress, falsely claiming Saddam Hussein possessed weapons of mass destruction and promising that toppling him would bring peace and democracy to the region.

These claims were lies. The war killed over a million Iraqis. And yet, politicians from both U.S. parties echoed Netanyahu's message almost word for word.

Why? Because through organisations like AIPAC, millions in campaign donations, and tightly managed media messaging, Israeli government priorities were seamlessly woven into the bipartisan consensus. Party leaders—Democrats and Republicans alike—rallied around a war that served foreign strategic goals, not the interests or safety of the American people.

When power is concentrated, donor-dependent, and whipped into ideological conformity, the party system becomes a tool open to capture by any elite force strong enough to buy access—even a foreign one.

Even the world's only superpower is not immune. When lobbies speak louder than citizens, and both parties read from the same script, democracy becomes theatre—and war becomes policy.

True democracy requires more than ballots. It requires the permanent decentralisation of power—ensuring that no individual, no ideology, and no party can launch war without scrutiny.

Only when power is dispersed, debated, and publicly accountable does war become difficult—and peace, finally, becomes durable.

In theory, political parties offer voters meaningful choices—contrasting visions, ideological debate, different values. In practice, they function as two wings of the same bird of prey. Whether branded left or right, most parties serve the same entrenched interests: arms manufacturers, intelligence agencies, financial lobbies, and media conglomerates.

When war is on the agenda, they flap in unison.

- The invasion of Iraq? Bipartisan.
- The war in Afghanistan? Spanned five administrations.
- Libya? Marketed as humanitarian, supported by both Republican hawks and liberal interventionists.
- Ukraine? Flooded with arms, money, and bipartisan cheerleading.

The electorate may change its preference. The war machine never pauses.

The Iraq War was not a partisan mistake. It was a bipartisan fraud. Sold with fabricated intelligence and media hysteria over non-existent weapons of mass destruction, the invasion received support from both Democrats and Republicans in the U.S., and from Labour and Conservative leaders in the UK. It led to the deaths of over a million Iraqis, destabilised the entire region, and gave rise to ISIS.

And the consequences for those responsible?

None.

George W. Bush paints watercolours. Tony Blair tours lecture halls. The intelligence officers who manipulated public opinion now appear on news panels. There were no tribunals. No resignations. No justice.

Vietnam? A near-identical pattern. The Gulf of Tonkin incident—used to justify escalation—was a fabrication. Declassified documents and the Pentagon Papers revealed that leaders knew the war was unwinnable. But they kept sending troops. Kept drafting teenagers. Kept bombing villages. Not because it made sense, but because admitting defeat would damage party credibility.

Afghanistan? A twenty-year occupation that cost trillions, achieved nothing, and collapsed in a week. Every president—Bush, Obama, Trump, Biden—perpetuated the myth. Not one told the truth. Not one was held accountable.

The lesson is clear: unaccountable power, as it now operates under the party system, has always—and will always—silence truth and bury the innocent. War becomes bipartisan theatre, truth an optional strategy, and the dead remain voiceless beneath a banner that claims to speak for them.

The result is a state of perpetual war. Not declared. Not debated. Just ... continuous.

- **Drone strikes in Yemen.**
- **Special operations across Africa.**
- **Proxy wars in Syria.**
- **Military bases encircling the globe.**

And through it all, the parties—on both sides—offer full support.

They change the slogans. They change the justifications. But the policies remain untouched.

Because the party system is not built to reflect the will of the people. It is built to manage them.

If you voted for peace and got war, you are not naïve—you are trapped.

If you marched against war and were ignored, you are not alone—you are disenfranchised.

Parties claim to listen to the public. But when war is waged on behalf of their masters, they ignore the people without hesitation.

The real decision is made long before any vote—by billionaire donors, intelligence officials, and unelected architects of empire.

These forces will not disappear with the end of the party system. But what will disappear is the machine that gives them cover—the apparatus that choreographs dissent, simulates debate, and maintains the fiction that the public was consulted.

In a No-Party democracy, every vote for war is visible, individual, and accountable. These interests may still try to interfere—but control becomes harder, corruption more visible, and betrayal directly punishable by the voters themselves.

War is not a failure of party politics. It is its product.

A system built on loyalty, hierarchy, and elite control cannot deliver peace. It delivers obedience. And as long as the war machine wears the mask of democracy, it will keep killing in your name—while the parties tell you it's what you voted for. If you want peace, you must do more than protest the war. You must dismantle the system that makes it possible.

In moments of crisis, people look to elected leaders for courage—for independence, for truth. But in a party system, courage is punished. Independence is crushed. Truth is optional.

The whip system—party discipline enforced through fear—is the velvet glove on the iron fist of party control. It is how wars are launched, lies upheld, and dissent suffocated. The whip's job is simple: to ensure party unity, no matter the issue, no matter the cost. And when the issue is war, the consequences become deadly.

- **It tells elected officials: your loyalty is to the party, not the people.**
- **It says: if your conscience objects, silence it.**
- **It says: if your voters demand peace, convince them they misunderstood.**

It reduces parliaments and congresses to echo chambers—where individuality is weakness and obedience is virtue. Where even the most consequential decisions, like sending a nation to war, are made not through thought, but through threat.

Careerism, Coercion, and the Cost of Conscience

When the U.S. Congress voted to authorise the war in Iraq, most members hadn't read the full intelligence. Many privately doubted the claims. A few knew they were lies.

But they voted "yes" anyway. Why? Because saying "no" meant isolation. It meant losing party favour. It meant being branded unpatriotic during a moment of national trauma. It meant facing donor retaliation, media attacks, and primary challenges.

In the UK, when Tony Blair pushed for war in Iraq, he made it a test of loyalty. Labour MPs who opposed the invasion were threatened with deselection, demotion, and political exile.

Those who resisted—like Clare Short or Robin Cook—were ridiculed, sidelined, or pressured into silence. In his resignation speech, Cook declared that he could not support a war "justified on the basis of intelligence that is still uncertain." The public applauded him. His party abandoned him.

In the days after 9/11, the U.S. Congress voted to grant President George W. Bush sweeping war powers. The vote passed: 518 to 1. That "1" was Barbara Lee. She stood alone and warned that unchecked military authority would lead to endless war. She was right.

But at the time, she was vilified. She received death threats. She was called a traitor. Her courage was historic. Her isolation was engineered.

When elected officials contemplate defiance, they're reminded of the costs:

- You'll lose your committee seat.
- You'll lose donor support.
- You'll be smeared in the press.
- You'll face a primary challenger.
- You'll never be re-elected.

The message is clear: vote with your party, or you're finished. And so, one by one, even those with doubts fall in line. The courage to say "no" to war is replaced by the calculation to say "yes" to survival. And history, once again, is written in blood.

Now imagine a system with no whips. No party offices. No donor pipelines. No threats of expulsion for thinking independently. In such a system, each representative is elected not as a soldier of a faction, but as a free agent of their community.

No one tells them how to vote. No one punishes them for asking questions. No one can strip them of their post for doing what is right.

In a No-Party democracy:

- **A vote for war is a personal decision, not a party strategy.**

- Every representative's stance is visible—clearly, directly, without spin.
- Cowardice has nowhere to hide. But neither does courage.

In this structure, the kind of moral clarity shown by Barbara Lee or Robin Cook wouldn't be the exception. It would be the norm. Because when the cost of war is measured in lives, the vote to go to war should cost everything. Not nothing.

The whip system is the executioner of democracy. It kills conscience before the bombs fall. It transforms elected chambers into rubber stamps for elite agendas. And it ensures that war—no matter how unjust, how unpopular, how false—always finds enough votes to pass.

To stop the next war, we must dismantle the party system itself—shatter the whip, break the bloc, and return decision-making to independent representatives who are free to vote with conscience.

We are told that democracy is government by consent. That when the people speak, leaders must listen. That public opinion is the ultimate check on power.

And yet, time and again, the people say "no" to war—and the war goes ahead anyway. Why? Because the party system was never built to reflect the will of the people. It was built to manage it. To contain it. To override it when necessary. Especially when the bombs start falling.

Iraq 2003: The World Said No—The Parties Said Yes

On February 15, 2003, millions of people across the globe marched against the impending invasion of Iraq. From London to Madrid, Rome to Sydney, São Paulo to Seoul—the world rose as one. It was the largest anti-war protest in human history. Over 1.5 million people flooded the streets of London alone. Polls showed a clear majority in Europe, Latin America, and parts of the U.S. opposed the war.

And yet, the invasion proceeded. Not because the facts changed. Not because the threat became real. But because the decision had already been made—by party elites.

- **In the U.S., Republicans and Democrats rallied behind Bush.**
- **In the UK, Tony Blair ignored his public, his intelligence community, and members of his own Cabinet—pressing forward with Conservative support.**

The Vietnam War tells the same story.

Public opposition began in the mid-1960s and grew louder each year. Students, veterans, clergy, and workers filled the streets demanding peace. By 1968, a majority of Americans believed the war was a mistake. And still it continued—for seven more years. Why?

Because the war was never about democracy. It was about obedience—not to the people, but to the empire behind the curtain. The Democrats under Johnson and the Republicans under Nixon may have taken turns at the podium, but they answered to the same masters: the military-industrial complex, corporate donors, Cold War ideologues, and the intelligence establishment. For them, the colour of the party didn't matter—as long as the killing continued and the contracts flowed.

The people lost their sons and daughters, their trust, and their hope.

The parties came and went—swapping faces, dodging blame, and obeying orders.

But their masters had it their way from start to finish—untouched, unaccountable, and utterly indifferent to the cost in blood.

In 2011, NATO launched a "humanitarian" assault on Libya. It ended with regime change, civil war, open-air slave markets, and total collapse.

There were no protests on the scale of Iraq. The public had learned: mass mobilization means nothing when both parties agree.

In Israel's repeated bombardments of Gaza, large swathes of Western publics express opposition or unease. But bipartisan support flows regardless.

When Consent Is Manufactured, and "No" Means Nothing

How is it possible for so many voices to be ignored? For public opposition to be so easily brushed aside?

The answer is systemic.

- Party control over media ensures anti-war voices are marginalised or mocked.
- Party discipline punishes dissenting politicians, pushing them out or silencing them.
- Party funding systems ensure that donors—especially those with defence contracts—have more influence than a million protesters.

In this system, elections become rituals. Public opinion becomes noise. Policy remains untouched by the outrage it provokes.

The people do not consent. They are manipulated. Are they also complicit?

Lulled by mainstream media headlines—headlines shaped by the same elite that controls the parties? Yes. But people will be people. Not everyone will become a political expert. And that's not a failure—it's human nature.

The problem isn't that the public is imperfect. It's that the system is built to exploit that imperfection—to manipulate, divide, and pacify.

A No-Party democracy doesn't rely on every citizen becoming an expert. It relies on something more realistic: electing individuals who are, in most cases, better informed, politically literate, and directly accountable to the people.

This doesn't guarantee perfect outcomes. But it does guarantee that elected representatives are no longer bound to obey party leaders, donors, or predetermined lines. And that when the people say "no," it can no longer be ignored.

We're told that, if we dislike what our government does, we can simply vote them out. But who do we vote for when every major party supported the war? Who do we choose when anti-war candidates are denied media access, starved of funding, and smeared as extremists?

When war becomes a bipartisan project, democracy becomes a dead letter. The ballot box offers no escape when the same bombs fall no matter who wins.

Now imagine a political system in which:

- **There are no party leaders to whip votes.**
- **No factions to enforce discipline.**
- **No central offices channeling donor influence.**

In such a system, public opposition would matter—because there would be no apparatus designed to override it.

- **A million protesters couldn't be ignored.**
- **Public outcry would directly threaten the career of an MP.**
- **War would require evidence, debate, and justification.**

And most wars, unable to meet those standards, would never happen at all.

Only when representatives are free—truly free—to reflect the will of those who elected them can we ensure that "no" means no, and never again becomes a whisper drowned out by the drumbeats of war.

In modern democracies, wars are not declared. They're sold. They are packaged, branded, and broadcast. Fear becomes a campaign. Lies become headlines. And when the dust settles, the architects of war vanish, while the public is left with nothing but coffins, amputations, and confusion.

At the centre of this machinery is the alliance between parties, media conglomerates, and lobbying interests. This unholy trinity manufactures consent—not just for war, but for every elite agenda disguised as policy.

And it is the party system that holds it all together.

In 1961, President Dwight D. Eisenhower warned of the growing "military-industrial complex"—a system where weapons manufacturers and military elites would exert undue influence over public policy. What he didn't predict was that political parties would become the primary delivery mechanism for that influence.

Today:

- Defence contractors bankroll both major parties in the United States.
- In the UK, firms like BAE Systems maintain cosy ties with both Labour and Conservative MPs.
- Lobbyists draft legislation, ghostwrite speeches, and host private briefings with top party officials.
- Retired generals become media pundits. Ex-ministers become consultants for weapons firms. Think tanks push pro-war narratives with undisclosed donors.

The result? War becomes bipartisan—not because it is necessary, but because it is profitable. It's not that both sides agree because the evidence is overwhelming. It's that both sides have been bought.

The Media Doesn't Report War. It Markets It.

The press was once called the fourth estate—a watchdog against state power. But under party rule, it becomes something else: a narrative manager. And when the state wants war, the media doesn't investigate. It amplifies.

- **Iraq's WMDs? Uncritically repeated by The New York Times, the BBC, and every major broadcaster.**
- **Syria chemical attacks? Framed as fact before any investigation concluded.**
- **Afghanistan nation-building? Portrayed as noble, even as internal memos admitted it was a farce.**

Judith Miller at *The New York Times* helped push the WMD myth. She faced no real consequences. British tabloids labelled anti-war MPs "traitors." Dissenting journalists were fired, smeared, or quietly dropped from mainstream coverage. This is not journalism. It is crisis marketing on behalf of power.

Every war has its chorus of "experts." They appear on television, write op-eds, speak with authority, and cite intelligence. But who are they?

- **Many are former military or intelligence officials.**
- **Many are funded by arms manufacturers, fossil fuel companies, or foreign governments.**
- **Most are ideologically aligned with ruling parties and help shape their messaging.**

The appearance of debate is just that—appearance. You're allowed to argue over how to bomb, when to bomb, or which weapon to use. But you may never question whether bombing should happen at all.

The power of the party system lies in its ability to coordinate.

- A few leaders decide the message.
- Party-aligned media outlets echo it.
- Think tanks reinforce it with pseudo-analysis.
- Dissenters are framed as fringe, naïve, or dangerous.

This isn't a conspiracy in the shadows. It's a chorus in the spotlight. And they're all singing from the same script.

The public, surrounded by this wall of curated noise, begins to believe that war is necessary. That the threat is urgent. That disagreement is unpatriotic. That silence is safer than asking questions. By the time the bombs fall, most people are too exhausted, too overwhelmed, or too misinformed to resist. They have been told:

- "We must act."
- "We have no choice."
- "They hate us."
- "It's about freedom."

And when the truth emerges—when the weapons aren't found, the regime doesn't fall, the people don't cheer—it's already too late. The war is history. The profits are banked. The parties have moved on to the next crisis.

Consent was never freely given. It was manufactured.

In a No-Party system, this entire apparatus begins to collapse.

- There is no central party to coordinate the message.
- Representatives stand independently, answering only to local constituents.
- Donors cannot channel money through party treasuries to buy messaging influence.
- Media outlets can't rely on party briefings to shape their coverage.

In such a system:

- **Debate is genuine. Dissent is common. Whistleblowers are protected.**
- **War narratives must survive open scrutiny.**
- **Journalists once again fear being wrong.**

If war is the most extreme use of state power, then it should be subjected to the most rigorous form of democratic scrutiny. Yet in party-run systems, scrutiny is suppressed, dissent is punished, and decisions are concentrated in the hands of those furthest from the consequences.

The architecture of party politics shields those at the top and insulates them from the human cost of their decisions. Representatives invoke loyalty to party, deference to leadership, or trust in selective intelligence to justify their votes. Responsibility dissolves into collective fog.

A No-Party democracy changes this. To authorise military action, a leader must persuade a majority of independently elected representatives. Each must review the evidence, consult their constituents, and vote without fear of demotion or party backlash. The vote becomes personal, visible, and subject to real scrutiny. Every representative owns their decision. If the war is unjust, they are answerable. If the evidence collapses, they cannot defer blame.

No-Party democracy does not promise utopia. People remain imperfect. Nations will still disagree. But when every decision must be defended in full view of those it affects, the incentives change. Representatives who wish to be re-elected must listen to their communities.

No-Party democracy doesn't guarantee peace. But it makes war harder—not just politically, but structurally. And in a world that has grown too used to killing in the name of politics, that alone is a monumental leap toward real democracy.

Chapter 5

The Politics of Division

How Parties Turn People Against Each Other

In a truly democratic society, ideological diversity should be a sign of vitality, a reflection of a population thinking freely, debating openly, and disagreeing without fear. But in the United States and other so-called democracies, what passes for ideological diversity is little more than a carefully choreographed performance—a theatre of opposition designed not to inform, but to inflame.

Here, political polarisation isn't an accident. It's a product—manufactured, marketed, and sold by the very institutions that claim to protect democracy. The Democratic and Republican parties have not simply diverged; they have calcified into rival corporations competing not for truth or justice, but for dominance over a captive electorate. What the public receives is not a robust exchange of ideas, but a branding war between two monopolies. Red vs. Blue. Us vs. Them. Always Them.

The effect is chilling. In this rigged game of political tug-of-war, voters are not invited to think. They're pressured to choose a side. Instead of engaging with nuanced policies or independent candidates, citizens are reduced to colour-coded pawns, herded into ideological enclosures with slogans, soundbites, and fear. What was once a democratic process has become a tribal ritual, where identity replaces inquiry, and loyalty is prized over logic.

This isn't just political theatre—it's structural warfare. The very architecture of the system is designed to entrench this division. Take the creation of so-called "safe seats." These aren't accidents of demography; they're products of manipulation. District lines are redrawn like battlefronts, using data and algorithms to engineer outcomes before a single vote is cast. Gerrymandering is not just a strategy—it's a scalpel in the hands of elites, carving up democracy into predictable parcels of power.

In these zones of political certainty, real competition is dead. Why court the centre when the fringe guarantees re-election? Why listen to all constituents when the base alone holds the keys to office? Representatives become echo chambers for their own team, radicalised not by belief but by calculation. The result is a Parliament of partisans, not a House of the People.

This rigging of the game is not limited to America. Across the Atlantic, the United Kingdom offers a haunting reflection. The First-Past-the-Post system may sound quaintly British, but its effects are anything but benign. Here, elections are routinely won without a majority of votes. Party whips enforce obedience like military commanders. MPs toe the line not because it's right, but because disobedience means career suicide. Even when their constituents cry out for representation, MPs often lower their heads and vote with their party—not their people.

What emerges in both cases is a grim parody of democracy—a system where allegiance is rewarded, dissent is punished, and independent thought is smothered beneath the iron curtain of party unity.

The polarisation we live with today—this ever-deepening chasm between left and right—did not erupt like a storm from the sea. It was built, brick by brick, over decades. Sculpted by party strategists and pollsters who learned that fear mobilises better than hope, that division wins elections, and that the surest path to power is to convince the public that the other side is an existential threat.

Without parties constantly rallying their base and demonising the opposition, the incentive to turn disagreement into permanent tribal warfare disappears.

Presidential and prime ministerial candidates, too, are far more likely to be moderate—chosen by representatives of the people rather than party elites, and required to cast a wide net to earn the support of a genuine majority.

Under the party system, debate becomes theatre. Nuance is mocked. Every issue—immigration, healthcare, gun laws, education—is reframed not as a policy challenge, but as a battle for the nation's soul. "You're either with us, or you're against us." Compromise becomes treason. And truth? Truth becomes malleable—shaped to serve the tribe.

This weaponisation of issues is not just cynical—it is corrosive. Take immigration: a complex, deeply human issue reduced to a shouting match about walls and open borders. Or gun rights, transformed from a conversation about safety into a symbolic last stand for freedom. Healthcare—a matter of life and death for millions—is portrayed either as a sacred right or a socialist invasion. These are not debates. They are spectacles designed to keep people angry, afraid, and distracted—because a divided nation is easier to control.

The 2020 U.S. presidential election was a masterclass in this manipulation. Out of fifty states, thirty-eight voted exactly as they had for the past two decades. The illusion of choice vanished under the glare of electoral maps soaked in red and blue. True contestation came down to a few swing states—Arizona, Georgia, Michigan, Pennsylvania, Wisconsin. A handful of battlegrounds decided the fate of 330 million people. This isn't democracy—it's roulette. If you don't live in a swing state, your voice is background noise.

And it's not just about the presidency. As of 2020, fewer than 14% of congressional districts in the United States were considered competitive. The rest? Locked down. Secured. Predetermined. Politicians no longer campaign to earn your trust—they inherit your vote by default. Incumbents are protected like precious relics, not held accountable as public servants. The cost is immense: voter apathy rises, trust in the system collapses, and civic participation becomes a hollow ritual—a box ticked in a rigged performance.

And yet, parties continue to manufacture crises. They cast every election as a final battle between good and evil—"a fight for democracy," "a war for the nation's future." These phrases may stir the heart, but they poison the mind. They leave no room for difference, no patience for dissent. They demand absolute loyalty—or else.

Identity as a Weapon—How Parties Hijack the Self

Political parties are no longer just vehicles for policy—they are machines of identity construction. They don't simply ask for your vote; they demand your soul. To belong to a party today is not just to agree with a platform—it is to adopt a worldview, a tribe, a moral compass. Disagreement is no longer perceived as difference; it's interpreted as betrayal.

Political scientist Lilliana Mason names this dangerous fusion the rise of *mega-identities*—the merging of political affiliation with race, religion, class, geography, and cultural values. These are not random alignments; they are cultivated fault lines. Carefully drawn, relentlessly inflamed. When who you vote for becomes who you are, disagreement becomes existential. A neighbour with a different opinion is no longer just wrong—they're a threat to your values, your family, your nation.

This is the territory of *affective polarisation*—a concept Mason explores with chilling clarity. It's the emotional charge that now fuels political life. People no longer oppose policies—they despise each other. Studies show that members of opposing parties hold each other in deeper contempt than ever before. They are less willing to hire, date, live near, or trust those from "the other side." And they don't even need to know what those others believe—their hatred is based on identity alone.

This isn't just social media outrage. It's a civil cold war—engineered over decades by parties that thrive on fear, loyalty, and blame. A slow, relentless unravelling of the social fabric, one thread at a time.

And the parties love it. Because this emotional division is the glue that holds their power together. If they can convince you that your political identity is sacred, then they can control you without ever having to serve you. Loyalty is no longer earned—it's inherited. Criticism becomes heresy. And the more divided you are from your fellow citizens, the more dependent you become on your party to protect you from them.

This dynamic isn't just unhealthy—it's undemocratic. It punishes conscience and rewards conformity. It silences local priorities in favour of party narratives. And it ensures that power remains concentrated in the hands of a few party elites, while the people they claim to represent are reduced to cheering sections in an endless game of partisan warfare.

If division is engineered, it can be dismantled. If loyalty is manipulated, it can be reclaimed. And if democracy has been hijacked, it can be rescued—not by tweaking the party system, but by breaking free of it altogether.

A No-Party democratic model does not pretend that tribalism or emotional bias will disappear—human nature ensures they won't. But as political scientist Lilliana Mason has shown, it is the party system that fuses identity with ideology. A No-Party system dismantles that fusion. It doesn't eliminate disagreement—it reshapes it. Without parties anchoring our identities and fuelling tribal narratives, disagreement can return to being deliberation, not destruction. It erodes blind allegiance to party brands and fosters a political culture where issues can be debated more openly—and opponents are no longer seen as existential threats, but as fellow citizens with different views.

Imagine an election where party labels no longer appear on the ballot. Where voters are forced—for once—to look at the individual, not the colour of their rosette. Where ideas, records, and integrity matter more than slogans and tribal dog whistles. Without the shorthand of party identity, voters become investigators, not spectators. Candidates become advocates, not avatars.

The result? Broader appeal. Real outreach. Instead of pandering to a polarised base, candidates must speak to a wider spectrum of voters. They can no longer rely on demonising the opposition to win support—they must persuade, not provoke. This breeds moderation, fosters dialogue, and disarms the rhetoric of moral war. Elections shift from identity battles to issue-based contests—and politics starts to look like public service again.

And the change doesn't stop at the ballot box. Inside legislatures, the absence of party whips unleashes a kind of political oxygen. Representatives no longer vote according to commands barked down from leadership—they vote based on judgment, conscience, and constituency. Coalitions emerge not from tribal obligation but from common goals. Debates are no longer zero-sum brawls—they're opportunities for negotiation and shared progress.

Gerrymandering? It loses its teeth. When no party has a monopoly on a district, redrawing boundaries becomes a hollow exercise. The manipulation of borders loses its power when voter loyalty cannot be taken for granted.

New voices? They finally have room to speak. Without parties gatekeeping who gets funding, endorsements, or ballot access, independents and community leaders can emerge. The political marketplace becomes dynamic again—not locked down by the duopoly of two brands, but opened up to innovation, diversity, and genuine representation.

One of the great myths of the modern age is that democracy is protected by competition. But under the rule of political parties, competition is an illusion—and control is concentrated. Nowhere is this more obvious than in the toxic alliance between party machinery and special interests.

In a partisan system, influence is streamlined. Want to sway policy? Just buy the party. Fund the campaigns, sponsor the conventions, control the messaging—and you've purchased a government wholesale. It's efficient, yes—but it's not democratic. It's a cartel.

And the cost is paid not in currency, but in broken promises, abandoned communities, and silenced dissent.

A No-Party system breaks that chain of command. When candidates are unaffiliated and independently elected, the old playbook doesn't work. There are no central party committees to funnel donations through, no shared media consultants running coordinated smears. Influence operations become fractured, unpredictable—and exposed. Transparency becomes possible. Corruption becomes riskier. The price of control skyrockets—and for once, the people may actually outbid the lobbyists with their votes alone.

And then there's the media.

In a party-dominated landscape, media outlets function as megaphones for factional narratives. The airwaves are drenched in outrage. Each channel becomes a cathedral of confirmation bias. On one screen, your side is saving the world. On the other, it's committing treason. Truth is no longer pursued.

But strip away the parties, and the media loses its anchor. No more easy scripts. No more "left" vs. "right" panels shouting past each other. Coverage must recalibrate around issues, not ideologies. Viewers begin to encounter unfamiliar perspectives. Public discourse breathes again. The temperature lowers. Complexity returns.

And beyond the institutions—in homes, in workplaces, in neighbourhoods—something even deeper begins to change.

Without parties dictating identity, disagreement loses its toxicity. Political views become just that—views. Not threats. Not betrayals. People start to realise that their neighbour, their coworker, their in-law who sees the world differently isn't the enemy.

This is what No-Party democracy makes possible: a culture of engagement, not estrangement. A society where civic participation means more than casting a vote every few years—it means shaping communities together, even across disagreement. A place where the absence of parties doesn't create a vacuum, but a clearing—a space for something better to grow.

In a world dominated by parties, leadership selection is not about finding the best—it's about finding the most loyal. The most charismatic. The most bankrolled. The primary system, especially in the United States, turns the hunt for national leaders into a grotesque spectacle.

In a No-Party system, the circus of partisan primaries is replaced with a more deliberate, measured, and rational process—a process designed to protect the public.

Start with the highest office—president, prime minister, head of state. In a reimagined No-Party democracy, candidates for such roles are filtered through a stage of deliberation, nominated by independently elected representatives. These representatives select candidates based on merit, integrity, and national vision.

And then, once the finalists are selected through this filter of reason and accountability, the people vote. Not between extremes or manufactured personalities, but between competent leaders who have passed a test of judgment.

For state governors or city mayors, the No-Party model applies just as clearly. No intermediary stage is needed. Candidates appear on the same ballot, stripped of party labels. They are judged by their records, their plans, and their connection to the people they hope to serve. Of course, human greed and corruption can persist even in No-Party settings. But without party labels to shield bad actors or reduce elections to brand loyalty, the system offers fewer places to hide. Civic accountability becomes sharper.

And suddenly, something astonishing begins to happen.

The country stops lurching between extremes. The political class starts to look less like a caste and more like a cross-section of society. The rhetoric cools. The fear subsides. Competence rises.

Critics of No-Party democracy often throw up their hands and say, "But people will still disagree." Of course they will. Disagreement is the pulse of a healthy society. But there is a world of difference between disagreement and division—between debate and warfare. The problem is not ideological difference. The problem is the machinery that turns those differences into permanent scars.

Political parties are that machinery. They take ordinary variance—in belief, in experience, in values—and weaponise it. They funnel it into binary cages, brand it with moral absolutism, and then sell it back to us as democracy. They don't reflect our differences; they manufacture and manipulate them. And in doing so, they poison every institution they touch—the courts, the media, the schools, the streets.

But in a No-Party democracy, the temperature drops. The oxygen returns. Debate becomes possible without dehumanisation. Conflict becomes constructive rather than catastrophic. Instead of being locked into red and blue cages, citizens are free to vote across issues, to collaborate across differences, to seek truth without fearing social exile.

Without parties enforcing groupthink, voters reclaim their individuality. Without party whips punishing dissent, representatives reclaim their conscience. Without media echo chambers drawing lines in blood, the public square becomes a place of conversation again.

And the result is not a nation without politics. It's a nation where politics is no longer a proxy for identity, no longer a substitute for belonging. A place where a disagreement over taxes or immigration doesn't destroy friendships or families. A society where civic life thrives in town halls and schools, not just polling stations. Where leadership is earned, not bought. Where complexity is not feared but welcomed.

Because democracy doesn't need parties to survive. It needs people—thinking, engaged, unchained people.

It would be naïve to expect everyone to abandon their distractions or suddenly break free from social media echo chambers. But people respond to the incentives their systems create. When the structure no longer rewards tribal outrage but instead values transparency, conscience, and accountability, behaviour begins to change.

Under a No-Party system, the entire civic ecosystem can shift. Education can finally be freed from ideological control and reshaped to foster critical thinking, tolerance, and genuine civic awareness. The media, no longer tethered to party narratives, is liberated to cover real issues—not just fuel outrage or pit one group against another. When the underlying structures change, so do the messages people receive, and eventually, so do the people themselves.

In the end, it's simple: the more we build our politics around parties, the more we divide ourselves. The more we strip those parties of their institutional power, the more we can rebuild what matters—trust, truth, and the fragile but precious fabric of a shared public life.

It's not too late. The path is hard, but it is clear.

Break the binary. Dismantle the machinery. Reclaim democracy from the party system that hijacked it—and return it to the people who were always meant to own it.

Chapter 6

Trojan Democracy

How Political Parties Enable Foreign Rule

THE GREAT DECEPTION of modern politics is not just that we are free, but that we believe we are the ones holding the pen of history. We wave flags with pride, recite national anthems with reverence, queue solemnly at the ballot box, and call it self-government. Every election is treated like a festival of freedom—speeches broadcast, debates staged, manifestos printed, promises performed. And through it all, we are told: *this is democracy.*

Behind the bunting and ballot slips lies a more insidious truth: sovereignty, in many nations, is a beautifully crafted illusion.

Power no longer sits with the people—if it ever did. Instead, it's whispered in foreign capitals, traded in closed-door meetings, and scripted in think tank boardrooms. And the conduit of this control? Not tanks. Not treaties. But political parties.

Yes—the very institutions we are taught to believe represent us are often nothing more than Trojan horses. Built to resemble the voice of the people. Hollowed out to carry the will of empire.

Gone are the gunboats of old. Today, conquest comes cloaked in consultation. Control arrives through campaign finance, election monitoring, party training sessions, and "democracy promotion" programs. Political parties—once imagined as instruments of public will—now function as the central pipelines through which foreign powers inject their interests into the bloodstream of sovereign nations.

Capture one party, and you capture the state. Fund one candidate, and you rewrite the nation's future.

This is not some distant conspiracy. It is empire reinvented—conquest without the chaos, occupation without the optics. The genius of modern imperialism is its subtlety: the people vote, but the outcome was negotiated before the first slogan was even printed. The actors change. The script does not.

But who writes the script?

Not the struggling farmer. Not the overworked nurse. Not the displaced worker or the disenfranchised youth.

The script is penned by foreign donors, intelligence agencies, multinational corporations, and the consultants who wine and dine with the party elites. The result? A puppet show with real consequences—where national sovereignty is rehearsed, not realised.

In the 20th century, as Africa, Asia, and Latin America raised their flags in triumphant ceremonies of so-called independence, the old powers quietly exhaled—not in defeat, but in satisfaction. The rifles had been traded for reports. The governors replaced by advisors. The whip exchanged for a wire transfer.

Where once rule was imposed by force, it now arrived through softer instruments: IMF structural adjustment programs, World Bank loans, NGO partnerships, and foreign-funded electoral "reforms."

The trap was elegant.

You may elect your leaders—so long as they embrace free trade, privatise public goods, suppress labour unrest, and keep the doors open to foreign investors. You may write your constitution—so long as it resembles Westminster or Washington. You may form parties—so long as their ideas remain within the narrow bandwidth of Western-approved discourse.

France never let go of West Africa—it simply continued to print its currency. Britain never severed its hold on the Middle East—it just dressed its influence in business suits and military contracts.

And the United States? It inherited the imperial throne, ruling not by flag but by fiat.

Belgium may have formally left the Congo, but the ghosts of Leopold's empire still haunted every corridor of power, every shattered dream.

To be clear, this is not an indictment of political parties as conscious actors, nor of the general populations in colonising nations. The parties themselves—whether in the former colonies or the imperial centres—are not inherently power-hungry. They are passive machines, structures through which power is exercised. It is the ruling elite, not the party or the nation, that steers these machines toward domination. Once captured, parties become the perfect tools—giving imperial ambitions a legal framework, a democratic façade, and a local face. The exploitation does not flow from the will of the people, but from elite interests manipulating institutions to serve a global agenda.

But who are these elites? In today's world, they no longer wear crowns—they hold board seats, defence contracts, and oil concessions. They operate through the financial systems that fund wars, the corporations that profit from them, and the political consultancy firms that script the justification. These elites include transnational oil companies, weapons manufacturers, intelligence agencies, global banks, and private equity interests whose fortunes depend on open markets, pliable regimes, and perpetual instability in resource-rich regions. The invasions of Iraq, the toppling of Mossadegh in Iran, the destruction of Libya, and the proxy war in Syria—all bear the fingerprints of an elite class whose true loyalty lies not with any nation, but with power itself. Wars are not declared in moments of open debate—they are engineered long before the vote. Through think tanks, media narratives, and party policy platforms, the case is manufactured. By the time it reaches parliament, representatives are whipped, dissent is marginalised, and legality is secured—all to give premeditated violence the appearance of democratic consent.

And these parties? They were cut-and-pasted from colonial models—artificial structures with no roots in local customs, no memory of ancestral governance, no connection to the fabric of everyday life. They spoke foreign ideologies in foreign tongues, judged legitimacy by foreign applause, and viewed Western grants, media praise, and NGO alliances as the highest badge of success.

To lead a party was not to represent the people—it was to win approval from abroad. To win an election was not to earn trust—it was to secure backing from embassies and economic forums.

And when parties refused to obey? When they spoke too boldly of national dignity? When they bent their knees to the people rather than the foreign masters? They were eliminated. Quietly, or with fire.

The graves of Patrice Lumumba in Congo and Mohammad Mosaddegh in Iran are not just tombs—they are warnings. Warnings that popular legitimacy means nothing if it threatens empire.

Guatemala, Chile, Congo—their histories are scarred by the blood of leaders who dared to lead for their people, not their patrons. And always, their replacement was ready: a loyal party, a foreign-trained candidate, a platform that sounded just enough like "reform" to be palatable to Western ears.

In this new age of velvet conquest, tanks are inefficient. Boots on the ground are messy. Occupation draws too much attention. But a party—hungry for cash, desperate for exposure, centralised and easy to hijack—is the perfect instrument of quiet control.

Especially in post-colonial and transitional states, political parties are born fragile. They lack deep roots. They hunger for foreign validation. And their leaders are often willing to trade principles for press coverage, loyalty for loans, sovereignty for sponsorship.

The playbook is simple. And devastating.

1. Identify the faction that's pliable. The "opposition" party that talks of "modernisation," "stability," and "international norms."

2. Fund it—quietly. Through think tanks, NGOs, capacity-building programs, foreign media partnerships.
3. Control the narrative. Elevate your allies as "reformers." Paint their critics as "autocrats," "populists," or "extremists."
4. Coach the candidates. Foreign embassies host PR workshops. Intelligence services train campaign teams. Donor advisors shape the messaging.
5. Sabotage the resistant. Economic sanctions. Currency manipulation. Media disinformation. Civil society unrest stirred like a pot on cue.

It is regime change by algorithm, by headline, by grant. Not by gunfire. Not yet.

Today's think tank is yesterday's spy agency in a new outfit. Capacity-building seminars are often just foreign-funded indoctrination camps. Election monitors preach transparency abroad while ignoring billionaire-funded circus elections at home. Foreign-backed "civil society" groups act as pressure valves. Media funded by "democracy aid" parrots slogans written continents away. "Independent" NGOs function as lobbying arms for ideological agendas.

Even the language is rigged:

> "Pro-democracy" means pro-Western.
> "Populist" means disobedient.
> "Autocrat" means unwilling to surrender sovereignty.

And the party system—by design—makes all of this seamless.

Because parties are built for obedience. Their hierarchies ensure that capturing a few leaders gives you the whole machine. Their funding structures allow foreign money to shape entire campaigns through legal loopholes and donor proxies. Their ideological branding makes it easy to pick winners and label losers—before the first vote is cast.

And let us not pretend this is only foreign interference. Domestic authoritarians have also mastered this architecture. The same party machinery used by imperial agents is used by despots to consolidate power, silence dissent, and build dynasties. Whether in Turkey's AKP, China's Communist Party, or Egypt's NDP, the political party is not a conduit for the people—it is a weapon wielded against them.

What colonial governors once enforced with batons, party leaders now enforce with press releases. What military juntas once controlled with tanks, modern regimes now manage with televised speeches, loyalty oaths, and press conferences broadcast on foreign-funded channels. The coup no longer arrives at midnight. It arrives with a press badge, a grant agreement, and an electoral toolkit. It doesn't break down the door. It walks through the front.

Let us now step out of theory and into blood-soaked reality. Into the shattered streets where flags of "freedom" flutter over ruined homes. Into the places where democracy is not a destination, but a disguise. Because in nation after nation, political parties have not delivered self-rule—they've delivered foreign dominion in local packaging.

As former CIA officer John Stockwell revealed after resigning in protest, the United States—while preaching democracy—was systematically undermining it across the globe. Stockwell confessed that the CIA had overthrown dozens of democratically elected governments, manipulated elections in countless others, and armed ethnic minorities to foment internal conflict. "We created civil wars," he admitted. "We funded opposition, rigged ballots, and trained death squads—all in the name of stability." But the stability they sought was not for the people—it was for elite economic interests. And just as elections were weaponised abroad, so too were the media and institutions at home—conditioning the American public to see imperialism as benevolence and coups as liberation. In truth, the democracy promoted by the West often stops at the border—and even within it, remains an illusion when real power is threatened.

Ukraine: Revolution by Design

In 2014, the world watched Maidan Square erupt in flames—protestors waving EU flags, chanting slogans of freedom, demanding change. The media called it a revolution. The hashtags exploded. Western leaders applauded.

But behind the chants and cheers, a quieter story was unfolding.

When President Viktor Yanukovych rejected an EU trade deal in favour of closer ties with Russia, it wasn't just a domestic decision. It was a geopolitical mutiny—a refusal to toe the Western line. And so, what began as genuine unrest was rapidly overtaken by foreign orchestration.

Billions had already poured into Ukraine under the banner of "civil society development." NGOs were groomed. Opposition parties were trained. Media outlets were funded.

And before Yanukovych had even fled, U.S. diplomat Victoria Nuland was caught on a leaked call choosing his successor. "Yats is the guy," she said—referring to Arseniy Yatsenyuk, a safe, Western-aligned technocrat.

This wasn't revolution. It was regime change in real time—project-managed with press releases and diplomatic nods. Ukraine got new elections. New parties. New slogans. But the puppeteers stayed the same.

The state became a battleground—not just between Ukrainian factions, but between empires vying for control. And the party system became the arena through which that war was waged. Parties for NATO. Parties for Moscow. Parties for IMF packages. Parties for oligarchs.

The people could vote. But they could not choose peace. They could not choose sovereignty. They could only choose sides.

Turkey: From Generals to Puppets

Once ruled by the cold hand of a secular military, Turkey's deep state ensured that no government would dare deviate from its Western-aligned, NATO-loyal trajectory. But then came Recep Tayyip Erdoğan, riding a wave of religious conservatism and economic promises.

To the West, he seemed perfect: moderate, market-friendly, pragmatic. But Erdoğan's rise was no solo act. It was made possible by the Gülen movement—a sprawling, U.S.-based Islamic network with tentacles in Turkey's judiciary, police, and education system.

Together, Erdoğan and the Gülenists dismantled the military's grip. The generals were purged. A new order took root—one backed by the very same foreign-linked institutions that claimed to champion democracy.

But alliances made in Washington rarely last. By 2016, the old partners had become bitter enemies. A failed coup attempt—widely believed to be driven by Gülenist factions—gave Erdoğan the perfect excuse. Tens of thousands were arrested or fired. Judges. Soldiers. Teachers. Journalists. The foreign-aligned networks were cast out. And in their place? An even tighter grip. Erdoğan became a one-man regime—still holding elections, still maintaining parties, but with no real opposition left.

He once declared himself co-chair of the U.S.-sponsored Greater Middle East Initiative. Today, he rules a country where sovereignty has changed hands many times—but never belonged to the people.

Egypt: The Revolt That Wasn't Allowed

Tahrir Square. 2011. A dictator falls. A people rise. The world watches.

Egypt was meant to be the success story of the Arab Spring. And when Mohamed Morsi, a civilian and member of the long-banned

Muslim Brotherhood, won Egypt's first free election, many dared to believe the future had arrived. But that future was never authorised. Morsi was immediately suffocated. Media attacks. Fuel shortages. Stalled loans. Orchestrated unrest. And finally, a military coup—wrapped in the language of "stability."

General el-Sisi took power. The U.S. resumed its aid. The West applauded the "return to order." Elections continued. Parties were allowed. But nothing changed.

Morsi's presidency lasted just over a year. El-Sisi's repression has lasted over a decade. The party system, once imagined as the path to freedom, became the cage in which hope was strangled.

Pakistan: Democracy on a Leash

"From the beginning, Pakistan's politics have alternated between civilian rule and military dominance—but behind every government, the real power has remained constant: the military-intelligence elite, backed and bankrolled by the United States."

Leaders rise—and fall—within the narrow corridor of what is *acceptable*. Zulfikar Ali Bhutto. Benazir Bhutto. Nawaz Sharif. Imran Khan. Each soared to popularity. Each, at one point, dared to step too far outside the script. Each was punished.

Imran Khan's story is the most recent and perhaps the most revealing. Initially embraced as an outsider with clean hands, he soon began speaking out against foreign interference and military control. That was the line he was not allowed to cross.

What followed was textbook: Party defections. A no-confidence vote. Criminal charges. Arrest. Protests were crushed. Media was silenced. Elections continued—but only for candidates with the right sponsors.

Pakistan's democracy isn't broken. It's tethered—kept alive just enough to fool the world, and dead enough to serve those who pull the strings.

The party system is the imperialist's dream: a ready-made infrastructure for soft domination, a polished corridor for influence, a Trojan horse that opens itself. But what happens when that door won't open? When a nation refuses to play along? When there is no party willing to kneel, no candidate who will obey, no opposition that can be bought?

Then the smiles vanish. And the missiles begin to fall. When foreign control cannot arrive through the ballot box, it comes through the bomb bay.

Libya: Democracy at the Barrel of a Gun

Muammar Gaddafi was no liberal saint. He ruled with an iron fist. But he was sovereign—proudly, defiantly so. He rejected U.S. military bases. He nationalised Libya's oil wealth. He funded pan-African institutions. He proposed a gold-backed dinar to free Africa from the dollar's grip. That alone sealed his fate.

In 2011, cloaked in humanitarian rhetoric, NATO unleashed a bombing campaign on Libya. The stated goal? "Protect civilians." The real objective? Eliminate the last truly independent leader in North Africa.

Suddenly, armed opposition groups—many tied to jihadist networks—were crowned "freedom fighters." Media outlets framed chaos as progress. Western leaders beamed about a "new chapter in democracy."

Gaddafi was captured. Tortured. Executed in the street. And Libya—once one of Africa's most developed nations—collapsed overnight. Open-air slave markets emerged. Civil war erupted. Jihadist militias ran wild. Three rival governments claimed control. And only after the ashes cooled were political parties reintroduced—aligned, of course, with foreign interests.

Bashar al-Assad was no champion of freedom. But he ruled a state that refused to bow. He aligned with Iran and Hezbollah. He rejected Israeli and American dominance. He governed without a party system that could be easily hijacked from abroad. That made him untouchable by soft power—and thus a target for hard power.

As early as 2006, Western intelligence agencies were strategizing regime change. According to Columbia professor **Jeffrey Sachs**, the goal was clear: dismantle Assad's government and rewire Syria's alliances.

When protests broke out in 2011, the floodgates opened. The **CIA launched Operation Timber Sycamore**—funnelling billions in arms and training to rebel groups, many of whom later empowered jihadist factions. Foreign fighters surged in. Allies like **Turkey, Qatar, Israel, and Saudi Arabia** joined the fray.

Airstrikes devastated infrastructure under the guise of anti-terror operations. Over **600,000 dead**. Millions displaced. A cradle of civilisation reduced to rubble.

And through it all, Western powers insisted they were supporting "democratic forces." But those forces were largely **Western-funded coalitions in exile—parties-in-waiting**, manufactured for the power vacuum that never quite came.

Eventually, Assad fell. In late 2024, Damascus was captured by rebel forces led by Hay'at Tahrir al-Sham (HTS), and its leader—Abu Mohammad al-Jolani, now using his birth name Ahmed al-Sharaa—was declared interim president of Syria. Once the leader of al-Qaeda's affiliate in the region, Jolani had been rebranded by the West as a "moderate." The same man once blacklisted as a terrorist had become the face of a Western-aligned Syria.

In May 2025, U.S. President Donald Trump met with al-Sharaa in Saudi Arabia, offering public recognition and announcing the lifting of sanctions. Washington, which had spent decades fighting terrorism in name, now embraced one of its former icons—as long as he served the right geopolitical function.

However, the conflict did not end with regime change; it only changed shape. Israel had intensified airstrikes in Syria, including a high-profile attack near the presidential palace in Damascus in late May 2025. Justifying its actions as protection of the Druze minority and pre-emptive defence, Israel's real motives appeared tied to reasserting regional dominance and shaping post-Assad Syria to its liking.

Turkey, which had supported the rebel government, condemned the strikes as a violation of Syrian sovereignty. Ankara had begun negotiating defense agreements with Syria's new leadership and warned against any foreign occupation or fragmentation of the country. Tensions between Turkey and Israel were rising, with Turkish and Israeli fighter jets reportedly coming into close contact in disputed airspace.

The power struggle was no longer simply internal. Syria had become a chessboard for regional and global powers, each seeking to mould its future—not for the sake of Syrians, but for their own strategic gain. The lesson was scorched into the earth: Refuse a manipulable party system, and the only option left is destruction—or replacement by one that can be managed.

The pattern is as tragic as it is undeniable: where there is a party system, it is captured; where there is resistance, it is destabilized; and where resistance proves too stubborn, too sovereign—it is bombed.

The suffering extends far beyond the millions of innocent lives lost and the devastation inflicted on countries like Iraq, Syria, and Libya. Western Europe, too, is facing the consequences—not only in the form of wasted taxpayer money, but in the fallout of a refugee crisis.

Refugees poured into Europe not because they wanted to abandon their homes, but because those homes were destroyed. They risked everything—their lives, their children's futures—because staying meant death or destitution.

Across Syria, Iraq, Libya, and Afghanistan, more than 15 million people have been forced to flee their countries as refugees—not counting the tens of millions more displaced within their borders. This is one of the largest human displacements of the 21st century, and it is not a natural disaster. It is policy made visible.

Now, it is Western Europe—the very societies whose elites championed or enabled these wars—that must grapple with the aftermath. Communities struggle to integrate the displaced. Public services strain. Political divisions deepen.

But these are not random crises. They are the long shadow of foreign policy shaped in boardrooms, not ballots. Without those wars, most of these people would never have left. And without elite-driven militarism, this chain of suffering—from Tripoli to London, from Kabul to Berlin—would never have been set in motion.

And the cost doesn't end with bombs or borders. For decades to come, these shattered nations will struggle to rebuild not just their infrastructure, but their very capacity to function. Education systems collapse. Skilled workers flee. Children grow up amid trauma and rubble, not classrooms and opportunity. These are not just destroyed countries—they are stolen futures.

This is not merely collateral damage—it is a strategic outcome. A population stripped of opportunity, divided by chaos, and reliant on foreign aid is far easier to exploit than one that stands educated, united, and sovereign.

In a No-Party democracy, this tragedy becomes much less likely.

There would be no single strongman to demonise, no manufactured dictator to topple in the name of "freedom." Power would be decentralised—shared across independently elected representatives from all communities. In countries like Syria, for example, this could include minorities such as the Druze, Kurds, Alawites, and Sunni Arabs. Foreign powers would struggle to justify bombing a system in which all factions have a seat at the table and a share of real power.

Occupation, regime change, and proxy war rely on binary narratives: good vs evil, democracy vs dictatorship. But a **No-Party model defies those binaries**. It disperses power, dissolves elite capture, and leaves no easy puppet to install—or to remove.

That is why No-Party democracy is not just morally preferable. It is strategically **resilient**—a defence against foreign domination and civil collapse alike.

The Western imagination is haunted by dictators. It sees them in every foreign capital: clenched fists, grey uniforms, snarling speeches. It tells itself a simple story—that tyranny reigns, that the people suffer in silence, and that all it takes is a spark of freedom to bring the whole system crashing down.

But this is a fantasy. And worse—it is a damaging lie. Because in much of the world, loyalty to a strongman is not a symptom of brainwashing, ignorance, or Stockholm syndrome. It is a rational response to a much darker history. It is a shield—battered, imperfect, but still standing—against something far more destructive than domestic repression: foreign domination.

After the 9/11 attacks, General Wesley Clark—former NATO Supreme Allied Commander—walked into the Pentagon and was handed a classified memo that stunned him. It outlined a chilling plan: the United States intended to "take out seven countries in five years." Iraq, Syria, Lebanon, Libya, Somalia, Sudan, and Iran—all targeted for regime change, not because of terrorism or imminent threat, but as part of a broader imperial blueprint. "We're going to start with Iraq," he was told, "then take out Syria and Lebanon, then Libya, then Somalia and Sudan, and then finish off Iran."

These were not defensive wars. They were offensive restructurings of the world order—coordinated not by democratic will, but by unelected strategists and elite interests, exploiting the machinery of party politics to keep the public distracted while entire nations were dismantled.

The wars would be sold to the public through fear and manufactured consent. But what Clark stumbled upon was not a defence plan—it was a demolition order for sovereignty across the Global South.

This is why millions across the Middle East, Africa, and beyond rally behind strongmen. Not because they love authoritarianism. But because they have seen what follows when the strongman falls. Not democracy. Not freedom. But chaos, bombs, and puppet governments.

In the post-colonial world, memory is not something archived in books. It is a scar that lives in the bloodstream. People remember what liberation by foreign powers *really* looks like. They remember the lash and the ledger. They remember the mines, the plantations, the starvation wages and the bayonets. They remember **how "civilisation" came wearing chains.** And they remember more recent atrocities too:

- Iraq—where "liberation" brought disintegration, torture chambers, and endless war.
- Libya—where "freedom" arrived by missile, leaving behind open-air slave markets.
- Afghanistan—where two decades of occupation collapsed in weeks, leaving a shattered state and a haunted people.
- **Syria—where a foreign-backed proxy war dismantled the state, fractured its unity, and left foreign powers dividing territory and extracting resources**

When you've seen what Western regime change really brings, you do not dream of Western democracy. You fear its arrival. And so you cling—not because you are blind, but because you can see too clearly.

In such a world, the authoritarian ruler—for all his flaws—does not rise because people are blind to his cruelty. He rises because they've seen what comes when he falls. He becomes, in the minds of many, not a hero but a shield—the last, imperfect barrier between their country and foreign conquest masquerading as liberation. The loyalty he commands is not born of love. It is born of experience. Of broken promises and stolen futures. Of watching foreign-backed opposition movements ride into town waving the banner of "democracy"—only to hand the country over to bankers, generals, and multinationals.

The politically conscious—those who have seen this pattern play out before—are not fooled. They know the difference between a reformer and a proxy. They know when a protest begins in the streets—and when it begins in an embassy. They have seen revolutions uploaded to Twitter before the first stone is thrown. And so, faced with this grim binary: A ruler who censors, but protects. Or a coalition that promises freedom but delivers foreign looting, many choose what seems like survival.

This is not a defence of tyranny. It is a reckoning with the conditions that make tyranny seem like the only defence. Because until the alternative is real—until sovereignty, dignity, and reform are not seen as mutually exclusive—millions will continue to cling to the devil they know, not out of loyalty, but out of logic.

Western discourse loves simple moral tales: Democracy vs. dictatorship. Good vs. evil. Freedom vs. fear. But real life is messier. And in much of the world, the choice is not between liberty and repression—it is between **internal control** and **external conquest**.

And so yes, many do choose the strongman. Because **he speaks their language.** Because **his soldiers, however brutal, are still their sons.** Because **his rule, however flawed, is not a foreign occupation repackaged as humanitarianism.**

The West may call him a villain. But for many of his people, **he is the last crumbling wall between them and annihilation.**

If we want to talk about real democracy—not theatre, not branding, but actual people's power—then we must **start by listening to the people we claim to want to liberate.** We must understand that:

- Democracy cannot be delivered by drone.
- Freedom cannot be imposed through sanctions.
- Representation must rise from below, not be downloaded from abroad.

If the political party is the Trojan horse of empire, then the No-Party model is the reinforced gate—the barricade that keeps the puppeteers outside the palace walls.

Imagine, for a moment, a democracy with no parties. No centralised hierarchy to hijack. No ideological script mass-produced in Western boardrooms. No party whip cracking down on conscience.

Just a mosaic of independent representatives—chosen by the people they live among, accountable only to their own communities, untethered from tribal allegiance or foreign alignment.

In a No-Party model, power is not stacked like a pyramid—easily captured at the top. It is scattered, diffused, atomised across local constituencies. It becomes hundreds of small fires instead of one great bonfire—impossible to extinguish with a single gust of foreign wind.

Foreign influence, then, faces a new reality. It cannot purchase control through a single party or platform. It must navigate a gauntlet of diverse, sceptical, independent voices—each rooted in a place, a people, and a personal mandate. What once required a single cheque now requires a hundreds of conversations. What was once bribery becomes a logistical nightmare.

This is why empires fear No-Party democracy—not because it's radical, but because it's inconvenient. It slows the machinery of manipulation. It disrupts the clean pipelines of ideological control.

In a No-Party democracy:

- There are no pre-packaged platforms to hijack.
- There is no opposition bloc to brand as the "pro-democracy alliance."
- There is no loyalist party to mould into a proxy regime.
- There is no party-aligned media arm to echo foreign slogans.

Instead, politics becomes beautifully chaotic—a noisy, pluralistic, friction-filled arena where every vote must be earned, not manufactured. Every representative must justify their choices not to a party boss, but to the people who trusted them with power.

No party line to hide behind. No donor cartel to answer to. No foreign "strategist" whispering in their earpiece.

What if the United States and the United Kingdom had been governed not by party machines, but by independently elected representatives—answerable directly to their voters, not to elite donors or party whips? Would they have been able to lie their way into Iraq—selling weapons of mass destruction that didn't exist, justifying a war that killed hundreds of thousands, and handing oil contracts to Western firms while Iraq burned?

In a No-Party system, the leaders would not have been agents of the war machine—elevated through party loyalty and corporate alignment. Nor would independent representatives have been herded into voting for war under the pressure of party discipline. The infamous "sexed-up" dossier—as it was called in Britain—could never have passed unchallenged through a chamber of unaligned minds, each accountable to constituents.

And if the media were truly independent—liberated from the same oligarchic interests that steer both policy and narrative—that dossier could not have been sold to the public either. A free press would have questioned, exposed, and refused to amplify deception. The march to war would have stalled not on ideology, but on accountability.

Would a No-Party system have allowed NATO to obliterate Libya—toppling Gaddafi not for human rights, but for daring to propose an African currency backed by gold? Would that war—masked as humanitarian—have succeeded if the governments waging it weren't entangled with financial, military, and oil lobbies that shape both their cabinets and their headlines?

And what of Haiti—where elected leaders are removed, assassinated, or undermined whenever they resist foreign control over mining rights or infrastructure? Would constant interference be so easy if Western powers couldn't act through obedient party blocs with pre-approved talking points?

These are not just past mistakes. They are recurring patterns—made possible by party-led democracies that centralise power, reward elite loyalty, and shut out dissent.

No-Party democracy might not have made Western leaders perfect—but it would have made it far less likely for those in power to be agents of the ruling elite. Imperial war would have been far harder to impose on principled, independent leaders by the military-industrial complex or neoliberal architects of a so-called "new world order." It would have been a harder sell to No-Party representatives, harder to coordinate without party discipline, and far harder to justify in the eyes of a public no longer fed scripted consensus through loyal media outlets.

Empires thrive when decisions are made by a handful of party elites. They would falter when decisions are made by hundreds of accountable minds. But there's another side to this story.

What if Iraq had been governed by a parliament of independently elected representatives—not a centralised regime that could be painted as a threat to the world? What if Libya had been a functioning No-Party democracy—with leaders accountable to their communities, not strongmen ruling by decree? What if Haiti's government wasn't made up of donor-dependent party elites, but local leaders with deep-rooted legitimacy and no backdoor to power?

Could the West have sold the same lies? Would the public in the UK and US have accepted the invasion of a sovereign country without the villain of a dictator to rally against? Would the media have so easily spun tales of liberation and democracy—if those nations were already more democratic than the ones bombing them?

The truth is this: Party systems on both sides—in the aggressor and the target—make war and exploitation easier. They offer a villain. They offer a vacuum. They offer a handle.

Remove the parties—and you remove the justification. You remove the façade of benevolent intervention. You remove the ability to disguise theft as liberation.

In the No-Party model, representatives are not courtiers competing for favour from a royal party hierarchy. They are jurors—each called to deliberate, each bound not by political loyalty, but by the people who sent them.

This doesn't mean every representative will be wise or virtuous. It means they are accountable—not to a party line, but to their constituents. If those constituents demand poor decisions, that is a failing of public will, not of structure. But what the structure does ensure is that no single agenda can be scaled across the nation without scrutiny, persuasion, and consent.

Unlike in party systems—where loyalty can override conscience, and whip-enforced discipline turns one faction's priorities into national law—No-Party systems fragment power by design. There is no bloc to control, no label to hide behind, no machine to enforce silence. Only individuals, each one required to make their case, face opposition, and stand openly by their vote.

And that is why jurors are harder to buy. Harder to blackmail. Harder to control. Not because human nature changes—but because the system does.

For decades we've been audience members in someone else's play. We've cheered for actors, not architects. We've debated scripts written in foreign capitals. We've cast ballots in a performance—not of democracy, but of manipulation.

These are not representatives. They are courtiers. Not citizens' champions, but branded functionaries in a travelling show of sovereignty. We are handed manifestos written by consultants. We are shown debates moderated by donors. We are told that our vote is power—but the menu has already been chosen, the ingredients imported, and the chefs trained abroad.

As long as political power flows through parties, it will be intercepted. As long as representatives answer to whips instead of their constituents, they will betray you.

As long as money speaks louder than communities, policy will be auctioned—to the highest bidder, whether oligarch or foreign sponsor.

No-Party democracy is a return to honesty—to deliberation, locality, and accountability. It is not perfect, but it is resilient. Not polished, but real. It fragments the power that parties centralise. It decentralises decision-making. It immunises our institutions from being turned into marionette theatres for foreign hands.

The people—at long last—must take the stage themselves.

Chapter 7

The Fourth Estate in Chains

*Political Parties and the
Death of Media Independence*

WHAT HAPPENS WHEN the watchdog of democracy is trained not to bark, but to heel? When the press—once feared by tyrants, once trusted by citizens—becomes a polished leash in the hands of political masters?

For decades, power has quietly traded hands behind a veil of "free press." Not from the public to journalists—but from journalists to corporate boards, and from corporate boards to political elites. The result is not a free media. It is a domesticated media—one that barks on command, bites only the powerless, and purrs under the touch of its real owners.

This transformation was not born of natural market forces. It was engineered—crafted through decades of legislative betrayal. Political parties, under the guise of reform, have dismantled the very laws that once protected journalistic independence. With surgical precision, they weakened antitrust regulations, permitted mergers, and ushered in an era of corporate media empires. Today, a handful of conglomerates dominate what we read, hear, and see—each with deep financial and ideological ties to the political establishment.

But this isn't just consolidation. It's colonisation. The media, once a wild terrain of investigative courage and dissenting voices, has been cleared and fenced, transformed into a plantation of narratives that serve the masters of wealth and office. Political parties, acting as agents of elite control, have ensured that this new media landscape silences rather than scrutinises—comforts power rather than confronts it.

Independent journalism hasn't merely been abandoned. It has been persecuted. Journalists who dare challenge the consensus—who dig too deeply into war, corruption, or corporate crime—are not defended by political actors. They are targeted, discredited, sued, or jailed. And the parties remain silent, because it is their order, their power, their illusion that must be protected.

What we now call the "mainstream media" does not reflect a diversity of thought. It reflects a unity of purpose—the survival of the ruling class. The press no longer informs the public; it trains it, pacifies it, keeps it busy. Not with truth, but with trivia. Not with scrutiny, but with spectacle. And not with dissent, but with fear.

The architecture of this control is not hidden. It was laid bare by Noam Chomsky and Edward Herman in *Manufacturing Consent*. Their model revealed five structural "filters" through which all news is strained—leaving only what serves the interests of the powerful.

- **Ownership:** The media is owned by billionaires and corporations whose fortunes depend on the status quo. They are not in the business of upsetting their friends in government or finance.
- **Advertising:** Newsrooms are funded not by readers, but by advertisers—powerful brands who frown upon any story that questions consumerism, capitalism, or elite corruption.
- **Sourcing:** Journalists are trained to rely on official sources—press secretaries, government briefings, corporate statements. Stray too far, and access disappears. Truth becomes a luxury.
- **Flak:** Challenge the narrative, and expect backlash—legal threats, public smears, job losses. Few dare persist.

- **Fear ideology:** From communism to terrorism, from pandemics to foreign propaganda—the public is kept in a state of fear, distracted from injustice at home by phantom enemies abroad.

These filters do not merely shape news—they shape *reality*. They decide what can be said, who can say it, and how it will be framed. They do not just marginalise dissent. They erase it—not with guns, but with silence.

One moment laid bare this collusion between parties and press: the Telecommunications Act of 1996. Sold as a reform for the people, it was in fact a gift to corporate America. Under its rules, giant media corporations were allowed to gobble up radio stations, TV channels, and newspapers—across markets, across platforms, with no concern for diversity or democracy. The landscape was cleared for empires like Clear Channel and News Corp to dominate public conversation with impunity.

This wasn't deregulation. It was political engineering—a strategic act by both Democratic and Republican parties to hand the microphone to the few, and mute the many. Those who played along were rewarded with flattering coverage. Those who dissented were drowned in noise, smeared as fringe, or quietly ignored.

And this silence—this carefully engineered silence—has had consequences far beyond newsroom walls.

The party-media alliance doesn't just control what gets amplified—it controls what gets erased. Today, the silencing of dissent is no longer a covert operation. It is brazen, public, and justified in the language of virtue.

Take the banning of RT (Russia Today) across Western nations. This was not done through public referendum, open court proceedings, or after a rigorous review of its journalistic record. It was executed with the stroke of a bureaucrat's pen—declared guilty of "disinformation," and wiped from the public sphere. No formal debate. No opportunity for counter-argument. Just erasure.

Was RT perfect? No. Like every state-affiliated media outlet, it had an agenda. But the question is not whether it had bias—all media does. The question is: was RT banned because it lied—or because it told truths that Western outlets would not dare broadcast?

This is not the behavior of a confident, open democracy. It is the behavior of a system that fears competing narratives. Ironically, this is precisely what the Soviet Union once did: during the Cold War, the Kremlin banned the BBC, Voice of America, and other Western broadcasters, labeling them as threats to the state. They, too, claimed it was about "disinformation" and "protecting public order." They, too, didn't trust their citizens to hear multiple sides and decide for themselves.

When Western governments adopt the same methods—banning foreign channels outright—they do not defend democracy; they imitate its enemies. They infantilise their populations, assuming that truth must be guarded, curated, and distributed only by approved sources.

In a world where BBC and CNN served as cheerleaders for wars based on lies—from Iraq to Libya—the standard for "truth" appears not to rest on accuracy or integrity, but on allegiance to the dominant narrative. The uncomfortable reality is that RT became dangerous not because it was false—but because it was uncontrolled.

Censorship dressed as virtue is still censorship. And when the response to competing information is to silence rather than to debate, it reveals not strength, but insecurity. Mature democracies should be able to withstand scrutiny—and even propaganda—without resorting to Soviet-style bans. Because once the precedent is set, it doesn't stop with foreign stations. It starts to apply to dissenting voices at home.

The same logic applies to TikTok—a platform demonised not for spreading falsehoods, but for being outside the control of Western elites. "National security," they cry. But what they fear isn't data theft. It's *narrative loss*. They fear platforms that might empower other voices—voices that do not parrot the party line.

The real threat posed by TikTok was never just Chinese ownership—it was narrative disorder. Unlike Facebook or Instagram, whose feeds are shaped by user networks, advertiser influence, and traditional media filters, TikTok's algorithm surfaced what young people were actually watching and engaging with—raw, emotional, unfiltered content.

During and after the 2023 Israel–Hamas war, TikTok saw a surge of pro-Palestinian content and sympathy from Gen Z. This sparked panic among political elites. Rep. Josh Gottheimer (D–NJ) accused TikTok of spreading "pro-terrorist propaganda" and demanded it be held accountable for "inciting hate." Rep. Mike Gallagher (R–WI) called it "digital fentanyl" and claimed the platform was "intentionally brainwashing" American youth. Jonathan Greenblatt, CEO of the Anti-Defamation League, went even further, saying TikTok was "like Al Jazeera on steroids," flooding users with "antisemitism and anti-Zionism with no repercussions."

It is no coincidence that shortly after this backlash, bipartisan support accelerated for legislation to force a ban or forced sale of TikTok—culminating in the passage of the Protecting Americans from Foreign Adversary Controlled Applications Act in April 2024. While the public justification focused on national security and Chinese ownership, the timing and tone revealed something deeper: a panic over losing control of the story.

When platforms no longer filter dissent—when young people are exposed to the consequences of foreign policy in real time—the manufactured consent begins to crumble. In such moments, the reflex of empire is not to reflect, but to reassert control—whether through bans, legislation, or censorship dressed as security.

A No-Party media ecosystem—like a No-Party democracy—is dangerous not because it is chaotic, but because it is honest. And in an age of digital power, honesty is what power fears most.

While dissent is banned under the guise of protection, the public is fed a steady diet of distraction. The airwaves are saturated with celebrity scandals, courtroom drama, sports controversies, and manufactured outrage. Real crises—wealth inequality, corporate criminality, ecological collapse—are buried beneath a mountain of noise.

Keep the people fixated on the trivial, and they will never look up. Keep them arguing over reality TV, and they won't ask who rigged the real game. This is bread and circuses, digitised and weaponised. The media has become a circus tent—full of flashing lights and dancing clowns—hiding the machinery of control behind its velvet curtain.

And when the curtain lifts, only briefly, the media's true allegiance becomes undeniable.

Nowhere was this clearer than in the run-up to the Iraq War.

The world watched in horror as the United States and the United Kingdom hurtled toward a war built on lies—claims of weapons of mass destruction that never existed. Millions marched in protest. Experts warned of catastrophic fallout. Whistleblowers risked their careers. But the media—the great Fourth Estate—didn't question. It *amplified*. It *cheerleaded*. It *manufactured consent*.

Networks parroted government talking points. Newspapers headlined false intelligence. Dissenters were painted as "unpatriotic," "radical," or "naïve." The media did not inform the public. It *inoculated* it—against doubt, against truth, against reason.

Journalist John Pilger called it what it was: "war by media." In his searing indictment, *The Triumph of Propaganda*, he exposed how journalism had ceased to be a check on power and had become its public relations wing. By 2013, most Britons believed fewer than 10,000 Iraqis had died in the war. The real number likely exceeded *one million*. The truth was not merely hidden. It was *scrubbed*—the blood washed clean by compliant headlines and forgetful coverage.

And what happened to those responsible for this grand deception? Were the editors fired? Were the broadcasters shamed? No. They were *rewarded*—with ratings, with access, with continued influence.

Even publicly funded broadcasters—the supposed last bastion of neutrality—are not immune. After the BBC dared to question the British government's war narrative, its Director-General, Greg Dyke, was forced to resign in 2004. The message was loud and clear—step out of line, and you will be crushed. Even the most "independent" institutions are not safe when political parties are the ones holding the purse strings.

Back in 1977, legendary journalist Carl Bernstein revealed that over 400 American journalists had worked with the CIA—knowingly or not—to push narratives favourable to U.S. interests. Major outlets like *The New York Times* and *Time Magazine* were implicated. In the UK, Richard Norton-Taylor of *The Guardian* exposed similar collaborations between British intelligence and the press. These were not exceptions. They were instructions—whispered into teleprompters and embedded in editorials.

Even now, more sophisticated tools are used to monitor and muzzle the press. Surveillance technology—once the realm of spy thrillers—is now standard operating procedure. Pegasus, the notorious spyware developed by Israeli company NSO Group, has turned journalists' phones into 24/7 surveillance devices. It doesn't just read your texts. It maps your movements, accesses your camera and microphone, and exposes your sources, contacts, and private thoughts. You are naked before the state.

This isn't speculation—it's documented. In 2021, more than 80 journalists from 17 media outlets across the world—coordinated by Forbidden Stories and Amnesty International's Security Lab—uncovered the scale of the Pegasus surveillance operation. Their investigation revealed that over 180 journalists in 20 countries had been selected as potential targets. These reporters faced threats, intimidation, and state harassment, not for what they had published—but for what they might.

Surveillance is no longer reactive. It is pre-emptive. It plants the seed of fear long before a whistleblower picks up the phone or a reporter opens their laptop. It warns them, silently: *we are watching*.

Even legal defence of this dystopian intrusion reveals how deeply power protects itself. NSO Group's legal representative? Cherie Blair—wife of former UK Prime Minister Tony Blair. In the theatre of democracy, the defenders of power wear respectable faces—and they call their spyware "national security."

As journalists like Laurent Richard and Sandrine Rigaud have shown, this isn't just about technology. It's about control—the ability to silence dissent not by confrontation, but by making you watch what you say before you've even said it.

This culture of intimidation is further buttressed by vague and sweeping anti-terror laws. Under the banner of "national security," journalists are detained, interrogated, and stripped of their tools. The laws say they're protecting the public—but the real target is truth.

Ask Scott Ritter, former UN weapons inspector and outspoken critic of U.S. foreign policy. He has faced constant legal and personal attacks, not because he lied—but because he *refused* to.

Control doesn't always arrive with sirens and subpoenas. Sometimes, it wears a suit, files paperwork, and smiles for the cameras. In the modern war on journalism, the courtroom has replaced the prison, and financial ruin is the weapon of choice.

This is the age of SLAPPs—*Strategic Lawsuits Against Public Participation*. These lawsuits are not filed to win. They are filed to exhaust, to intimidate, to crush. Their message is simple: speak out, and we will destroy you—not with truth, but with legal fees.

Take the case of Gawker Media. In 2016, the gossip site was sued by wrestler Hulk Hogan over a leaked sex tape. But behind the celebrity face was a far more chilling truth: the lawsuit was bankrolled by billionaire Peter Thiel, whom Gawker had previously exposed. This was revenge, not justice. And it worked. Gawker went bankrupt. Its journalists were scattered. A media outlet was wiped off the map—not by regulators, not by censors, but by one wealthy man with a grudge and the legal firepower to act on it.

Meanwhile, those who challenge power in the public interest are hunted like criminals.

Consider Julian Assange. Through WikiLeaks, he exposed war crimes, surveillance programs, and diplomatic hypocrisy on a scale never before seen. His reward? A decade of exile, imprisonment, and psychological torture. Charged under the Espionage Act, a law meant for spies—not journalists—Assange has become a living warning to anyone tempted to challenge elite power. His case is not about justice. It is about deterrence. *Expose the truth, and you will be broken.*

Chelsea Manning. Edward Snowden. Daniel Hale. These are not criminals—they are whistleblowers, punished not for lying, but for telling the truth. Their crime? Revealing what their governments were doing in secret. War crimes. Mass surveillance. Civilian killings reported as statistics.

The list is not long—and that's what makes it so telling. So few dare to expose the truth, because the price is exile, imprisonment, or lifelong persecution. In a system that claims to value transparency, those who reveal uncomfortable facts become enemies of the state.

The party system, regardless of ideology, closes ranks when its secrets are threatened. Red or blue. Tory or Labour. They may disagree on tax rates or slogans—but on one point they are united: the truth must serve them, not the people.

And yet, in this scorched landscape, there still exist pockets of defiance—small, underfunded, independent outlets that refuse to play the game. They publish stories the mainstream won't touch. They investigate corruption, war, surveillance, inequality. They are everything the press is meant to be.

They survive on crumbs: crowdfunding, donations, volunteer work. No corporate advertisers, no government subsidies, no party patrons. Just courage—and a ticking clock. Because one lawsuit, one algorithm change, one hack—and they're gone.

The promise of the internet once offered hope. For a fleeting moment, the walls trembled. Blogs, podcasts, and social media cracked the gates. Suddenly, anyone with a phone and a conscience could speak to the world.

But the party establishment didn't just sit back. They regrouped. They adapted. And they brought the old tools of suppression into the new digital arena.

Today, online discourse is governed by algorithms designed not for truth, but for engagement. Rage sells. Outrage trends. Complexity is buried. And the rules? They're written by a handful of tech titans, guided not by democratic values, but by profit and political pressure.

Content that exposes corruption? Buried. Videos that challenge NATO narratives? Demonetised. Accounts that question party orthodoxy? Shadow-banned or deleted. The same filters Chomsky and Herman warned us about—ownership, flak, ideology—now govern our digital world. Only now, they operate at machine speed.

Even billionaires are not immune. In late 2023, after Elon Musk allowed a freer range of expression on X (formerly Twitter)—including posts critical of Israel—major advertisers launched a coordinated boycott. Companies like Disney, Apple, and IBM pulled their ads, citing Musk's endorsement of a post they labelled antisemitic. But the broader concern was the platform's refusal to moderate political narratives in line with elite expectations.

At the *New York Times DealBook Summit*, Musk did not mince words. In one of the most explosive live television moments of the year, he said: "If somebody's going to try to blackmail me with advertising, blackmail me with money—go f* yourself. Go. F***. Yourself. Is that clear? I hope it is."**

He then accused the advertisers of trying to "kill the company" through economic coercion.

But it didn't stop there. X filed lawsuits against multiple organisations, including the Global Alliance for Responsible Media (GARM) and Media Matters for America, alleging that they had orchestrated an illegal advertising boycott designed to destroy the platform's revenue base. Musk argued that these groups weren't protecting public discourse—they were policing it on behalf of entrenched interests.

This wasn't about promoting safety or preventing hate. It was about enforcing conformity. Musk's case became the clearest proof yet that economic pressures can be wielded to silence platforms and individuals who deviate from dominant narratives—even in spaces that claim to champion free speech.

And when even the world's richest man can be publicly punished for refusing to filter truth through acceptable lenses, what hope is left for ordinary citizens?

Governments—or more precisely, the parties in power—don't just participate in narrative control; they enforce it. Not in defence of the people, but in service to the donors, corporations, and elite networks that keep them in office. Draped in slogans like "fighting disinformation" or "protecting democracy," they pressure platforms to silence dissent.

Censorship today rarely arrives with a black bar or a deleted post. It comes in whispers—through visibility throttling, shadow-banning, search suppression, algorithmic exile. Your voice isn't erased. It's buried.

And that's the point. In a digital world run by invisible levers, the most effective control is the kind you never notice. And through it all, the illusion of choice remains.

Flick through the channels. Scroll through the apps. A thousand voices, a million headlines—and yet, the message feels the same. Why? Because it is the same. Behind the façade of plurality lies the same architecture of control. A few corporations. A few donors. A few party machines. And an iron grip on the stories we tell ourselves.

The framing of reality itself has been hijacked. Poverty is not the result of structural injustice—it's a personal failing. War is not for profit—it's for freedom. Candidates outside the establishment aren't principled—they're "radical," "naïve," or "dangerous." Those who dare to say otherwise are cast out as cranks or foreign agents.

This doesn't just distort the news. It *distorts democracy*. The playing field is tilted long before a single vote is cast.

If democracy begins with the ballot, then the media decides who gets to appear on it—not in law, but in perception. And in a world shaped by parties and billionaires, that perception is tightly choreographed.

Candidates who serve the system are introduced with reverence: "seasoned," "moderate," "realistic." They're given airtime, glossy profiles, softball interviews. But those who challenge the power structure? They are caricatured from the moment they announce: "radical," "unelectable," "extreme." They are dismissed before a single debate. Ridiculed before a single policy is heard.

Bernie Sanders. Jeremy Corbyn. Both stirred mass democratic movements. Both exposed grotesque inequality, corporate greed, and war profiteering. And both were relentlessly undermined—not by public rejection, but by media assassination. Editors, pundits, and party operatives worked in unison to frame them not as threats to poverty or corruption, but as threats to *stability*. And the people—deprived of truth—were told to fear their own empowerment.

By the time voters reach the polls, the damage is done. The field has been narrowed, the terms set. It is no longer a contest of ideas. It is a selection of acceptable managers. A beauty pageant of the status quo.

And after the election? The media's grip tightens. News outlets don't merely report on governance—they *shape* it. They decide what is a "crisis" and what is "politics as usual." A collapsing health system? Shrug. A tax on billionaires? Catastrophe! A protest against war? Dangerous extremism. But drone strikes in foreign lands? Business as usual.

The boundaries of possibility are drawn not by public need, but by elite tolerance. If the media says reform is impossible, most people believe it. If they say war is inevitable, the tanks roll on. If they say the system works, who are we to question?

Even mass movements—surging with anger and hope—are quickly funnelled back into safe lanes. The media focuses on the loudest, most divisive voices. Coherent demands are ignored. Nuance is lost. Leaders are misquoted, ridiculed, or rebranded. The result? The movement is fragmented before it can become effective.

Coverage of elections has become a spectator sport—a horse race where policies are background noise. Who's up in the polls?

Who made a gaffe? Who wore what? Voters are treated not as decision-makers, but as fans cheering from the stands. Win or lose, the system wins—because the terms are never up for renegotiation.

And this circus continues after the votes are counted.

Day after day, the media defines the agenda. What gets airtime becomes policy. What doesn't fades into oblivion. Want to pass legislation? Convince the press it matters—or more accurately, convince the donors who own the press. This is the invisible hand that guides our politics: a media empire wired to party power, telling the public not what to think, but what to think about.

When the media declares economic reform "naïve," it becomes naïve. When it calls anti-war voices "unrealistic," they become unrealistic. When it repeats, endlessly, that "nothing can be done," it becomes a self-fulfilling prophecy.

But the greatest casualty in this arrangement isn't a candidate. It isn't a policy. It's the public's ability to imagine anything different.

In a healthy democracy, the press is the oxygen—informing, questioning, challenging. But under the rule of party systems, it becomes a sedative. It doesn't wake us. It lulls us to sleep. It whispers that this is the best we can hope for. That power cannot be moved. That the truth is too dangerous to know.

The greatest threat to elite power is not violence, but *informed consent*. An electorate that knows who pulls the strings. That sees through the spectacle. That demands answers and doesn't accept performance in place of principle.

That's why the truth is under attack. That's why journalists are surveilled. Why whistleblowers are jailed. Why media consolidation is tolerated—even encouraged—by parties across the spectrum. Because when the press becomes independent, the public becomes dangerous.

A truly free press cannot coexist with a party system built on control.

To reclaim democracy, we must first break the chains wrapped around our fourth estate. That means not only defending the brave few who still report the truth—but dismantling the structures that keep them marginal. Political parties are not victims of media decline. They are the architects of its captivity.

Until we sever this alliance—until we decentralise power, dissolve party control, and return journalism to its public mission—democracy will remain an illusion.

Because without a free press, *consent is manufactured*. And without real consent, *freedom is a lie*.

In a true democracy, the media is not a megaphone for power—it is a mirror held up to it. It is the public's shield against deception, their torch in the dark corridors of government. But in our world, that mirror has been shattered and replaced with a screen—carefully programmed by party strategists and corporate interests to tell us not what *is*, but what we must believe.

This distortion will not be corrected by media reform alone. Because the media is not broken in isolation—it is broken by *design*, by a political system built on factions, money, and manipulation. And to truly free the press, we must strike at the source: the party system itself.

A No-Party democracy offers more than just new faces and new voices. It offers a *new terrain*—one where journalism is not filtered through gatekeepers, punished for disobedience, or coerced into partisanship. In such a system, the media becomes dangerous again—but only to the corrupt.

In the party system, journalism walks a tightrope over a pit of silence. Reporters know that a single step out of line—a story too critical, a headline too bold—can mean losing access, losing funding, or losing their jobs. Editors are cautious. Publishers are political. And the press becomes less a watchdog than a lapdog, trained to flatter rather than to bite.

But imagine a system where that leash is cut. In a No-Party democracy, there are no parties to please. There's no longer a single power centre the press must court. No party office to anger. No leadership circle to fear.

Reporters are free to challenge each representative on the merit of their actions—not their loyalty to a faction. The chilling effect of party intimidation begins to thaw. And in its place, real journalism breathes again.

Under party rule, information flows through tight filters. Press briefings are carefully staged. Leaks are weaponised. In a No-Party system, there are no party spokespersons. No one to spin the narrative. No one to shield representatives behind press releases and talking points. Each representative speaks for themselves—and must answer directly to their constituents and the press.

Journalists gain access through initiative. There is no longer a central narrative manager—only elected individuals with nowhere to hide. Debates are no longer choreographed. Messaging is no longer dictated. And reporters are finally free to ask real questions.

This isn't chaos. It's clarity. It's real accountability. And it doesn't just change what the media covers. It changes how the public sees the media. When reporters challenge a representative, they aren't seen as partisan. They're seen as doing their job. And public trust in journalism begins to rebuild.

Under the party system, the media landscape is split like a battlefield. Red outlets and blue outlets. Left press and right press. Each one spinning the same event through different ideological lenses. Truth becomes relative. Facts become footballs. The result? Division, tribalism, paralysis.

A No-Party democracy breaks this binary. With no parties to align with, media outlets are freed from ideological gravity. They are no longer forced to "pick a side," because the sides themselves dissolve. Journalists are not punished for challenging one faction or another—because no faction exists to retaliate. Instead, they are free to explore the *full spectrum* of political thought, to challenge *any* representative, and to represent the *public interest*.

Reporters stop asking, "Will this offend the party?" and start asking, "Is this the truth?" Outlets stop competing for partisan market share and start competing on substance, depth, and relevance. Debate is no longer a shouting match between teams—it becomes a civic conversation among citizens. And most importantly, investigative journalism stops being framed as sabotage—and is restored as a public service.

In the world of parties, truth is dangerous—not because it's false, but because it's *inconvenient*. Whistleblowers are hunted not for lying, but for telling the public what the powerful want buried. And investigative journalists who dare amplify their voices are treated as enemies of the state.

Party systems are wired for damage control. When a scandal breaks, the reflex is immediate: close ranks, deny everything, discredit the source. It's not about right or wrong. It's about survival—of the party, the leadership, the illusion of unity. And in this battle for control, truth is the first casualty.

In a No-Party system, there is no central leadership to protect, no party image to defend. Each representative stands on their own record. Scandals are no longer collective liabilities—they are individual failures. And that means exposing corruption becomes not just safe—but politically useful.

Suddenly, investigative journalism is not a threat. It's a *service*. Whistleblowers are not pariahs. They are *heroes*. And the press is free to do what it was born to do: expose wrongdoing, wherever it hides.

Even the law shifts. In a party system, strong protections for whistleblowers and journalists are often blocked—because they threaten the party's ability to manage internal dissent. But in a No-Party framework, where power is decentralised and transparency is a competitive advantage, there is *political will* to protect truth-tellers.

This change is foundational. Because when the press is free to investigate—and whistleblowers are free to speak—democracy gains its spine.

One of the most insidious forms of media control is invisible: regulation. Party-run governments appoint loyalists to media oversight boards, weaponise defunding threats, and manipulate rules to suppress dissenting voices.

Public broadcasters may appear independent on paper, but behind the scenes, their leadership is often chosen through government-influenced processes. Step out of line, and the message is clear: we control your funding. We control your board. We control your future. In the United States, for example, public broadcasters like PBS and NPR have faced repeated threats of funding cuts when their reporting challenges the political agenda of those in power. The punishment is rarely direct censorship—it is structural pressure. Compliance is bought through budgetary intimidation.

But in a No-Party system, these levers of control are broken. Regulators are no longer appointed by victorious parties. Appointments are no longer spoils of power. Independent representatives are far less likely to support the selection of partisan or controversial figures. Without party blocs to push nominees through, consensus becomes essential—and with it, a higher standard of neutrality, competence, and public trust.

Moreover, prime ministers and presidents can no longer rely on a guaranteed majority of loyal party members to shield them. They cannot threaten oversight institutions without risking widespread backlash from independently minded representatives who owe them nothing. The cost of manipulation rises. The risk of backlash increases. The system becomes more resistant to coercion, not because individuals are better, but because the structure no longer rewards domination.

Public broadcasters, freed from party-linked leadership and funding threats, can finally become what they were meant to be: platforms for public service, not political survival. Editorial independence is no longer a slogan—it becomes a lived reality, protected by institutional design.

Censorship by funding fades. Propaganda by omission becomes harder to sustain. And for the first time in a generation, citizens can turn on their television or radio and expect to hear the truth—not a government-sanctioned version of it.

Party politics centralises power. And where power gathers, so too does attention. National outlets fixate on party clashes and capital scandals, drowning out the everyday realities of regional life.

Local journalism—once the heartbeat of civic engagement—is left to wither.

But a No-Party system reverses this dynamic. When representatives are elected as individuals, no community is expendable. No vote is taken for granted. Every neighbourhood becomes politically relevant—as a sovereign voice in a shared democracy.

In this model, local media isn't a hobby or a relic. It becomes the essential bridge between the public and those who represent them.

Independent candidates rely on local platforms to speak, explain, and be held accountable. Newsletters, podcasts, regional papers—once sidelined—become indispensable. And with that renewed demand comes revival.

Local journalists are no longer ignored. They are sought out. Local issues—housing, education, healthcare, policing—return to the fore. Through these local lenses, democracy begins to regrow its roots. Trust isn't rebuilt in televised debates or party conferences, but in town halls and school board meetings. Journalism becomes what it was always meant to be: a civic institution, embedded in the everyday lives of the people it serves.

In a No-Party system, journalism becomes what it was always meant to be:

- **A channel of direct accountability**
- **A tool of public education**
- **A safeguard against secrecy**
- **A platform for diversity, not division**

In this system, reporters don't chase scandals for partisan gain. They chase *truth* for public good. Media coverage reflects policy substance. Journalistic independence is seen as a cornerstone of democracy. The press is no longer a loyal opposition. It is a free people's sword and shield.

In a party-run system, the war on "disinformation" is just another war for control. Each party brands the other's truths as lies and demands censorship disguised as protection. Fact-checkers are distrusted not because facts don't matter—but because everyone knows the facts are filtered through partisan interests. In this fog of factional warfare, truth becomes collateral damage.

Party machines spin reality to protect their brand. Corporations distort evidence to shield profits. Foreign actors exploit division to destabilise rivals. And social media platforms, driven by engagement, amplify outrage, emotion, and tribalism—not clarity.

In a No-Party democracy, these incentives begin to break down. Without a party machine to defend or an opposition bloc to destroy, the incentive to twist truth for political survival weakens.

Politicians stand on their own record. There's no coordinated propaganda war to wage, no central narrative to protect. Disinformation becomes less useful—and less rewarded. Foreign interference also begins to lose its strategic logic.

A No-Party democracy that no longer engages in regime change, proxy wars, or covert interference abroad is harder to paint as an existential threat.

When a society is less polarised, there is less outrage to monetise. When voters don't see each other as enemies, the content that divides and enrages becomes less viral. Conspiracies still exist—but they no longer dominate the public square or win airtime in televised debates.

Importantly, even sensitive decisions—like vaccine rollouts—are more likely to follow rigorous scientific scrutiny, open debate, and public trust.

Of course, disinformation will never disappear entirely. There will always be people who believe that the Earth is flat, or that vaccines are part of a sinister plot. But the difference is this: under a No-Party system, the structure that fuels and legitimises political disinformation disappears.

A No-Party system could genuinely empower independent bodies—composed of journalists, scientists, technologists, and ethicists—to safeguard public discourse.

Today, online platforms are the new media gatekeepers. But unlike newspapers and broadcasters, their decisions are hidden in code. Algorithms decide what rises, what sinks, what spreads. Engagement trumps truth. Outrage outperforms accuracy.

A No-Party democracy redraws this terrain. Without centralised party power, platforms face far less political coercion. Political communication becomes dispersed—a mosaic of independent voices. This decentralisation weakens the influence of algorithmic bias. When power is scattered, manipulation becomes harder. Content rises not by affiliation, but by substance.

Transparency rules can also be strengthened. In a No-Party system, there is greater political will to regulate platforms in the public interest. Disclosure of algorithmic curation, political ad funding, and moderation decisions becomes not a threat to power, but a democratic imperative. And most importantly, space opens for alternative platforms—civic tech, local forums, decentralised tools—designed not to harvest data, but to foster dialogue. Public-interest communication becomes possible again.

The party-media system has done more than distort information. It has corroded culture. Cynicism is now common sense. Outrage is the new normal. Trust is a joke. Every issue becomes a tribal brawl. Every journalist is presumed biased. Every debate becomes performance art—designed not to persuade, but to enrage. This isn't politics. It's a psychological war, and the casualties are critical thinking, civic unity, and public faith.

Imagine a system where issues are not reduced to slogans, where debates are not framed as battles, where reporters are not seen as saboteurs. Where public trust isn't demanded—it's earned.

That's the cultural promise of No-Party democracy.

- **Young people *re-engage*—through town halls and transparent votes.**
- **Journalists are no longer caricatures—they are neighbours, watchdogs, civic partners.**

- Citizens speak with one another, in shared language, about shared problems, with shared stakes.

This is not utopia. This is recovery. The rebuilding of a political culture based on integrity—not identity. The party system has shackled journalism, not because it fears chaos, but because it fears accountability. To revive journalism, we must cut the chain at its source. Not just with media reform, but with political reformation.

In this new landscape:

- The press asks hard questions—and gets real answers.
- Broadcasters serve citizens.
- Investigative outlets thrive.
- Local reporters are front-line democrats.

And the public? The public stops being an audience. It becomes a force.

The restoration of the Fourth Estate is not about nostalgia. It's about survival—not of parties, but of democracy itself. Because without a free press, the people cannot rule. And without people's rule, there is no democracy.

Break the party system—and we break the spell.

Chapter 8

Justice Captured

When the Courts Serve the Powerful

The judiciary, once revered as the sacred cornerstone of justice in democratic society, has become a cracked foundation—fractured by the relentless pressure of political ambition. Courts were meant to be sanctuaries of fairness, the last line of defence between the individual and the state, the voice of principle in a room full of power. But in the hands of political parties, the gavel has become a weapon.

Across the world, political parties—aided and abetted by powerful elites—have seized control of legal institutions. Not to uphold justice. Not to protect the people. But to shield themselves, silence dissent, and punish opponents. The legal system, built to limit power, has been repurposed to entrench it. It's a quiet coup that hides behind robes and rituals, masked by the illusion of neutrality.

It begins at the source: the appointment of judges. In theory, this process should be guided by merit, wisdom, and integrity. In practice, it has become a partisan tug-of-war, where ideology trumps impartiality, and loyalty to the party outweighs loyalty to the law.

In the United States, Supreme Court nominations have devolved into gladiatorial contests—not over legal competence, but over political allegiance. Nominees are scrutinised less for their fidelity to the Constitution than for their reliability in delivering rulings that advance the nominating party's agenda. And once installed, these judges hold the power to shape law—and society—for generations.

Now imagine a legal system not used to seek justice, but to punish truth. A courtroom not as a temple of fairness, but as a trapdoor—sprung beneath the feet of those who dare to challenge power. This is lawfare: the calculated use of legal proceedings to bankrupt, silence, and destroy opponents. It is litigation as assassination.

Behind the scenes of modern democracy, powerful interests—corporations, billionaires, and elite lobbies—collude with party machines to deploy the courts like a phalanx of obedient soldiers. The lawsuits may be dressed in legalese, but their intent is blunt: to intimidate, isolate, and exhaust anyone who threatens the status quo.

These are not isolated incidents. They are systemic. And they are spreading.

Take the SLAPP—Strategic Lawsuit Against Public Participation. The name is clinical. The effect is chilling. Activists, journalists, and whistleblowers who shine light on corruption or ecological devastation are dragged into courtrooms and drowned in paperwork. These lawsuits are rarely meant to win. They're meant to wear down. The goal is to drain your bank account, your time, your resolve—until you stop speaking, stop investigating, stop resisting.

In the United States, environmental activists exposing pollution by oil and gas giants have been hit with wave after wave of defamation claims. Even when these suits are thrown out, the message is loud and clear: challenge us, and you'll pay for it.

One of the most infamous cases is that of Steven Donziger, the lawyer who secured a $9.5 billion judgment against Chevron for environmental damage in Ecuador. What followed wasn't a debate over facts—it was retribution. Chevron launched a relentless legal counteroffensive, aided by U.S. courts, that left Donziger under house arrest, disbarred, and financially devastated. This wasn't justice. This was corporate vengeance, sanctioned by a judiciary weaponised by party-aligned power.

This is how it works: the party protects the donor, the donor funds the lawsuits, and the courts become a theatre of repression. It's a triangle of control—and the public is the prey caught in the middle.

The chilling effect ripples outward. Journalists begin to self-censor. Whistleblowers stay silent. Civil society organisations tread carefully. The message is unmistakable: challenge the interests behind the ruling party, and you will face the cold blade of the law.

Meanwhile, political parties cash in. They secure campaign donations from grateful benefactors. They avoid media scandals by silencing their sources. They pass laws favourable to their allies while using the courts to break the backs of their critics.

The rule of law is supposed to be the great equaliser—the promise that no matter your wealth, your status, or your connections, justice applies to all. But in the world of party politics, that promise is a lie wrapped in ceremony. Behind the façade of fairness lies a ruthless double standard: one law for the people, another for the powerful.

Political parties in power wield the judiciary like a scalpel, cutting precisely where it hurts their opponents while sparing their friends. Prosecutors become political agents. Investigations are greenlit or buried based on party loyalty. Justice is no longer blind—it's got one eye on the polls and another on the donors' list.

We've seen this hypocrisy play out on a global stage. In the United States, whistleblowers who dare expose government crimes are prosecuted with ferocity, while those responsible for the crimes walk free.

Take Edward Snowden. He revealed that the U.S. government was illegally surveilling its own citizens—an egregious violation of the Constitution. For this act of public service, he was charged under the Espionage Act and driven into exile. Meanwhile, the architects of that mass surveillance program—shielded by their political affiliations and party protection—suffered no consequences. They retired with pensions and book deals.

The same tools that are weaponised against dissenters become invisible when allies of the ruling party commit offenses.

Corruption is overlooked. Misconduct is redefined. Accountability becomes optional—reserved only for the powerless.

This two-tiered system doesn't just break laws—it breaks faith. Faith in fairness. Faith in democracy. Faith in the idea that government serves all, not just the few with the right party badge.

It's a betrayal so deep that it doesn't just affect the courts—it infects the soul of a nation. People stop believing in justice. They stop voting. They stop caring. And when people give up on justice, those who crave unchecked power find the perfect conditions to thrive.

If war is politics by other means, then political prosecution is politics in a judge's robe. When courtrooms become campaign stages, and indictments replace debate, democracy has already begun to unravel. Ruling factions no longer need to win arguments or persuade voters—they need only outmanoeuvre their rivals in court.

Across the world, legal systems are increasingly weaponised to neutralise political opponents. Tanks and coups have given way to subpoenas, charges, and televised trials. The judiciary, once a check on power, is repurposed to eliminate threats, manipulate public perception, and tilt the electoral playing field.

In Brazil, Luiz Inácio Lula da Silva was convicted on contested charges and barred from running in 2018—a move widely seen as politically motivated. Though he later returned to power and now serves as president once again, the damage to democratic integrity had already been done. In Pakistan, Imran Khan was imprisoned ahead of a critical election cycle, coinciding with a military-backed reshaping of the political landscape. And in Russia, where authoritarianism is more overt, legal mechanisms are still used to create a façade of legitimacy—even as opposition leader Alexei Navalny was repeatedly imprisoned, poisoned, and ultimately died in custody.

These cases differ in context and severity, but the pattern is clear: the law is no longer neutral. It has become a partisan instrument—a means of clearing the field before voters get their say.

Even in the United States, the prosecution of Donald Trump became a global spectacle—and a constitutional stress test. To some, the charges represented long-overdue justice. To others, they looked uncomfortably like lawfare: the use of courts to sideline a political rival. Whether one supports or opposes him, the timing, intensity, and coordination of legal action raised concerns far beyond party lines.

And yet, despite it all, Trump is once again President.

His return to power, following one of the most aggressive legal campaigns in modern U.S. history, leaves behind a divided country and a damaged judiciary. If the goal was to protect democracy, did the prosecutions succeed—or did they undermine public trust in the justice system itself?

This is not about defending any one individual. It is about defending the principle that courts must never become extensions of political strategy. Because when prosecutions are perceived—rightly or wrongly—as partisan tools, democracy pays the price. Today it may be one man. Tomorrow it may be anyone who challenges the status quo.

In a truly No-Party system, where representatives are accountable to voters, these tactics lose their power. The courtroom becomes a place for justice again.

Julian Assange, founder of WikiLeaks, pulled back the curtain on war crimes, corruption, and government deceit. For this, he was hunted across continents. Charges were fabricated, dropped, resurrected—all in service of silencing a man who told the truth too loudly. His real "crime" wasn't publishing secrets. It was disrupting the narrative that political parties and their elite backers so carefully control.

Assange wasn't just punished. He was made into an example—a warning shot fired at every journalist, activist, and citizen who might dare challenge the system. His years of confinement, legal limbo, and isolation were not about justice. They were about deterrence.

This is what political prosecution looks like. It's not justice denied—it's justice inverted. It's the sword of the law plunged into the back of democracy itself.

The courtroom was once imagined as sacred ground—a place where justice stood above politics, where robes meant restraint, and where verdicts were guided by principle, not pressure. But under the rule of political parties, this ideal has crumbled into dust. Judges no longer rise above the fray. Too often, they are dragged into it—not as impartial arbiters, but as foot soldiers in a war for power.

In Hungary, Viktor Orbán's Fidesz party reengineered the judiciary into a partisan instrument. Through legislative sleight of hand and court-stacking, Orbán's regime turned the constitutional court into a rubber stamp—a shield for executive overreach and a bludgeon against dissent. The very institution meant to protect democracy became the scaffold on which it was hung.

In the United States, judicial appointments are no longer legal decisions—they are political campaigns. Entire swathes of federal judges are selected based on ideological predictability, not legal merit. Under both Democratic and Republican administrations, the Supreme Court has become an ideological battleground, issuing rulings that reshape civil rights, corporate regulation, healthcare, and elections—not according to the Constitution, but the preferences of the party that appointed them.

Once judicial independence is eroded, every other institution can be captured. Laws no longer protect—they persecute. The courts no longer check power—they cloak it. And public trust collapses as people realise that the law no longer serves them, only those who rule in their name.

If the weaponisation of the judiciary is a symptom, then political parties are the disease. Their hunger for control is not occasional—it is structural. Parties do not merely compete; they conquer. And once in power, they do not restrain themselves. They reach into every institution—the media, the civil service, the courts—and remake them in their image.

In today's party systems, judicial appointments function as strategic weapons. Executives and legislatures, driven by partisan interests, install judges who will carry their ideological banner for decades. Appointments to key positions—prosecutors, police commissioners, regulatory heads—are made with one overriding question: "Will they protect us?"

In such systems, the legal process is no longer a pursuit of justice—it becomes a tool of political warfare. Charges are filed to eliminate rivals. Investigations are launched not from necessity, but from strategy. Judges are celebrated when compliant, attacked when inconvenient, and quietly removed when they refuse to play along. The courtroom becomes a battleground, not a safeguard.

Examples abound. In Turkey, President Erdoğan—once jailed in 1999 for reciting a political poem—rose to power with the help of legal reforms and strategic alliances, including support from the secular opposition CHP. Its then-leader, Deniz Baykal, helped clear the path for Erdoğan's return to politics after his conviction. Two decades later, Erdoğan presides over a judiciary that critics argue has become an extension of executive authority.

Following the failed 2016 coup attempt, his government purged over 4,000 judges and prosecutors, claiming they were affiliated with the Gülenist movement. While infiltration was a legitimate concern, the scale and intensity of the purges raised serious questions about political opportunism and the collapse of judicial independence.

Today, that same judiciary is being used to prosecute Ekrem İmamoğlu, the popular Istanbul mayor and a leading CHP presidential contender—from the very party that once defended Erdoğan's democratic rights. İmamoğlu's charges, stemming from remarks allegedly insulting election officials, are widely seen as politically motivated. The irony is stark: Erdoğan, once a victim of judicial overreach, now presides over a system that uses the same tactics to crush his challengers.

In Russia, the courtroom has become pure performance. Judges wear robes, but speak with the voice of the Kremlin. Dissenting verdicts are virtually nonexistent. The law exists not to serve the ruled, but to shield the ruler.

In a No-Party system, the party lever is gone. No bloc can ram through judicial appointments using a manufactured majority. Without party machines, there are no ideological camps to align with—and no partisan lines to reward.

Instead, decisions are shaped by consensus across a chamber of independently minded representatives—individuals accountable only to their constituents. Appointments are judged not on political loyalty, but on competence, integrity, and public trust.

Legal actions with political implications must pass a higher threshold—not just of legality, but of legitimacy. They are no longer automatic responses to political threats, but deliberate actions, subject to public scrutiny.

In No-Party democracies, independent voices assess each case on its own terms. Some support. Others criticise. In that disagreement, truth has room to breathe. The courtroom becomes a space of argument again. A non-party legislature creates an incentive to expose injustice. Structural pluralism becomes a safeguard. If a prosecutor goes rogue, if a minister abuses power, if a judge plays politics—someone will speak out.

In such a system, judges are bound to the law. Their rulings are interpreted as legal arguments. Criticism still exists, but it's aimed at reasoning.

Over time, even existing institutions begin to function more effectively—simply because polarisation fades. Without a party to stack the bench, appointees are judged on merit. Loyalty tests lose their power. Hearings shift from performance to substance. Public confidence rises. As the culture shifts, so does the system:

- **Whistleblowers are less likely to be hunted.**
- **Prosecutors are less likely to rise through patronage.**
- **Judges are less likely to be threatened or bribed.**
- **The law begins to operate as a shield for citizens.**
- **It protects the powerless from abuse, not the powerful from consequence.**

Judicial independence cannot be declared into existence by decree. It must be grown—in soil free of factional warfare, executive dominance, or party capture. A No-Party democracy creates that soil:

- It removes the triggers that corrupt institutions.
- It disarms political incentives that turn courts into battlegrounds.
- It slows the reflexes of vengeance.
- It raises the bar for legitimacy.

And that's why the judiciary is one of the ruling party's most coveted prizes. Why? Because in the hands of a dominant party, the courts can accomplish what the ballot box cannot: eliminate rivals, silence critics, protect allies, and cement elite control under the cover of legality.

That's not judicial dysfunction—it's judicial capture. And it's no accident. It was engineered by the party system itself.

The solution isn't reform from within, but the abolition of the very structure that made that capture inevitable.

CHAPTER 9

The Illusion of Democratic Choice

*How Political Parties
Hijack Representation, Silence Dissent,
and Sell Us the Illusion of Freedom*

Across the Western world, from the marble halls of Washington to the green benches of Westminster, political parties parade as the engines of democracy—organising debate, guiding policy, giving the people a voice. But peel back the curtain, and a darker truth emerges. These parties do not reflect the will of the people. They manufacture it. They do not expand our choices. They curate them.

Whether red or blue, left or right, most parties in power operate under the same quiet consensus: protect the market, serve the donor class, contain dissent, and call it freedom. Elections become battles between nearly indistinguishable elites, each promising change while preserving the status quo. And the people—told they must choose the lesser evil—end up voting for the same cage, repainted every few years in new colours.

Across Western democracies, the parties that dominate public life no longer stand for fundamentally different visions of society. They stand for different marketing strategies serving the same system. In the United States, the Democrats and Republicans pretend to battle—yet both bow before Wall Street, expand the surveillance state, and vote for war after war. In the United Kingdom, Labour and the Conservatives trade insults in Parliament, but both enforce austerity, court corporate donors, and silence dissenting voices.

In France, the centre-left and centre-right shuffle power between themselves while maintaining EU-imposed fiscal orthodoxy. In Germany, grand coalitions between Christian Democrats and Social Democrats govern with dull predictability, united in economic conservatism and NATO allegiance.

The 20th century saw this slow merging of party lines. In the U.S., both parties embraced Cold War militarism, deregulation, and free-market dogma. The bipartisan consensus bloomed like a virus: invisible, adaptable, immune to election cycles.

In the U.K., the Labour Party was once a voice of the working class. But that voice was hijacked. Under Tony Blair's "New Labour," the party adopted Thatcherite economics, embraced privatisation, and rolled out the red carpet for Rupert Murdoch—the billionaire media mogul whose newspapers had long shaped public opinion in favour of conservative politics. Even the vocabulary changed—from solidarity to opportunity, from public service to private partnership. The result? A party that still wore the name "Labour" but served the same masters as the Tories.

In a true democracy, parties would compete to serve the people. In ours, they compete to serve the throne. The throne is not a royal seat—it's a metaphor for ruling capital: billionaire donors, multinational lobbies, foreign policy influence networks, and corporate conglomerates. These are the true powerbrokers, and political parties have become little more than auditioning servants, each trying to prove they will be the more loyal, more obedient, more useful steward of elite interests.

Consider AIPAC, one of the most influential lobbying groups in the United States. It funds candidates across both major parties—and those candidates compete visibly and enthusiastically for its approval. Joe Biden proudly declared: *"I am a Zionist. You don't have to be a Jew to be a Zionist,"* and has claimed he's done *"more for Israel than any U.S. president in history."*

Donald Trump, from the other side of the aisle, echoed the same loyalty—boasting that he was *"the best friend Israel ever had,"* after moving the U.S. embassy to Jerusalem, cutting Palestinian aid, and recognising Israeli sovereignty over the Golan Heights.

The bipartisan courting of AIPAC is just one example. The same dynamics play out across every major sector—defence, finance, fossil fuels, pharmaceuticals. Party leaders pitch themselves as the better investment. A more stable bet. A more useful tool.

In a No-Party system, there is no throne to serve. No party machinery acting as a go-between. Candidates stand on their own. If they grovel for power, it must be before their voters—not billionaires behind closed doors.

Once upon a time, parties were born out of movements—labour struggles, civil rights, constitutional reform. But today, they move to a different rhythm: the jingle of campaign donations, the whisper of lobbyists, the revolving door of corporate appointments.

In the United States, the illusion of democracy was buried beneath a flood of money. As campaign costs exploded, parties transformed into fundraising machines—addicted to corporate cash and beholden to the donor class. Lobbyists no longer waited in the wings. They wrote the scripts. They crafted the bills. They dictated the terms.

In 1971, the now-infamous Powell Memo outlined a corporate blueprint to recapture government, media, and education from the clutches of progressive reform. Over the next decades, business interests built think tanks, bought airwaves, and bankrolled both major parties. By the Reagan era, the takeover was complete. Deregulation, union-busting, and tax cuts for the ultra-rich weren't just Republican goals—they became bipartisan dogma.

Bill Clinton's presidency sealed the deal. NAFTA, welfare "reform," financial deregulation—policies that gutted the working class—were repackaged as centrist pragmatism. The Democrats didn't resist the corporate tide. They rode it.

Across the Atlantic, the U.K. followed suit. Under Blair, Labour ditched its working-class roots for City of London respectability. Rupert Murdoch was courted like royalty. Hedge fund donors walked through the front door. And policies once considered sacred—public ownership, trade union rights, universal benefits—were quietly euthanised.

The result? A political class shaped by—and for—its benefactors. No bribes required. The ideology of the elite had already become the default setting of government itself.

In any political system—capitalist, socialist, or anything in between—the institutions of state power determine the boundaries of possibility. They decide which voices are heard, which interests are served, and which futures are imagined. But these institutions do not stand alone. They are shaped, staffed, and steered by those who hold executive and legislative authority. And in modern democracies, that authority is exercised—and increasingly monopolised—through political parties.

This book does not seek to argue the merits of capitalism or state socialism. It does not prescribe a singular economic doctrine. Instead, it examines something more fundamental: who controls the apparatus of government, how that control is maintained, and why the current system prevents meaningful change—regardless of public will or economic logic.

At the centre of this problem lies the political party. What began as a mechanism to coordinate representation has become a gatekeeping device through which entrenched elites capture the lawmaking process and, by extension, every major organ of the state.

The sequence is not accidental. It begins with the capture of the executive—the government—by a party system that filters candidates, rewards conformity, and prioritises loyalty over independence.

Once executive authority is secured, party leadership—operating in the interests of entrenched elites—decides who advances within the system and who is excluded from meaningful influence.

From there, the machinery of state is gradually reshaped. Key institutions are staffed not for competence or impartiality, but for alignment with the dominant order. The party apparatus determines who may stand for election, what issues are permitted on the agenda, and how representatives are expected to vote—not based on evidence, conscience, or public interest, but in service to elite priorities. With this control over political processes comes the ability to enact legislation that entrenches power, neutralises opposition, and reinforces compliant sectors across society—including the media, the security establishment, and educational bodies.

What follows is a cascading effect: the quiet colonisation of the state.

- Intelligence agencies are filled with loyalists.
- Public broadcasters are transformed into instruments of narrative control.
- Police and military forces are subtly politicised, often through promotions, rhetoric, or strategic appointments.
- Education systems are directed toward producing obedient workers rather than critical thinkers.
- Regulatory bodies become passive or co-opted, serving private interests rather than the public good.
- And legal frameworks are restructured to protect the powerful, not the people.

None of this requires a formal authoritarian regime. It unfolds incrementally—through appointments, funding decisions, messaging coordination, and legal reforms—all under the outward appearance of democratic normalcy.

Elected leaders ascend via tightly controlled party ladders—designed to reward obedience, ideological conformity, and donor approval. And often, those who succeed are already compromised—entangled in networks of influence, favours, or secrets that make them easier to control. The now-infamous case of Jeffrey Epstein, whose private connections spanned multiple presidents including Bill Clinton and Donald Trump, illustrates how individuals vying for high office can be drawn into elite circles long before assuming public power.

Once in office, such leaders are not independent actors. They are stewards of continuity. Their role is not to challenge entrenched institutions, but to protect them—including intelligence agencies that resist transparency and operate beyond meaningful civilian reach.

This is why presidents change, but policies remain the same. Surveillance programmes continue uninterrupted. Covert operations proceed without pause. Whistleblowers are hunted, not heard. And bipartisan consensus ensures that the most secretive agencies face the least scrutiny.

The issue is not secrecy alone—it is impunity. Intelligence agencies are shielded by partisanship, overseen by compromised legislatures, and appointed by executives elevated through factional gamesmanship. Reforms, when they are proposed, are usually cosmetic. Real change would require dismantling the very structures that sustain the elite's grip.

This cycle only breaks when those enabling structures are dismantled. When party hierarchies no longer control access to power, the political culture itself begins to shift. Oversight becomes a civic obligation. Intelligence appointments require genuine consensus. Leaders must earn the trust of a politically diverse chamber.

This structural shift turns oversight from spectacle to substance. Whistleblowers become protected voices. Covert programmes face scrutiny not from one party investigating another, but from a plural legislature accountable to voters. And crucially, leaders can no longer appoint intelligence chiefs through backroom deals or ideological alignment alone. Appointments must pass through a chamber of independently elected representatives. The result? Fewer patronage appointments. More professional integrity. Far less space for partisan cronies to embed themselves in secretive, unaccountable roles.

This isn't utopia. But it is a tangible improvement—a transition from elite continuity to public oversight, from systemic impunity to democratic scrutiny.

The United States offers a stark illustration. For decades, agencies like the CIA and NSA have operated with near-total autonomy. Their surveillance infrastructure, covert operations, and foreign interference efforts were not born of a single administration—they span presidencies, protected by bipartisan loyalty and an embedded military-industrial complex.

Edward Snowden's 2013 revelations were not the exposure of a rogue programme, but of a bipartisan surveillance state. Initiated under George W. Bush, expanded under Barack Obama, and barely reined in afterward. Even when a president—like Donald Trump—expressed discomfort with certain interventions, the policies continued. Intelligence strategies proved indifferent to electoral change.

Why? Because intelligence agencies in party-based democracies are not beholden to voters—they serve enduring elite networks that cut across elections and outlast presidents. Their loyalty lies with defence contractors, private interests, and institutional survival.

Even John F. Kennedy—one of the most powerful U.S. presidents in history—was constrained by this machinery. After the Bay of Pigs fiasco, he famously vowed to "splinter the CIA into a thousand pieces and scatter it to the winds." He dismissed Director Allen Dulles and several senior officials—a rare act of presidential defiance. But reform never came. The CIA's power deepened, its budget grew, and its insulation from public accountability became more entrenched.

Whether or not the CIA or affiliated actors played a role in Kennedy's assassination remains speculative. But the aftermath spoke volumes. No president since has dared challenge the intelligence establishment so directly. The lesson was clear: these agencies are untouchable—not by law, but by consequence.

As long as party systems persist, this protection will endure. Presidents and prime ministers rise through hierarchies beholden to elite continuity. Lawmakers installed by party machines do not threaten the intelligence services—they shield them.

That is why reclaiming democracy cannot begin with ideology. It must begin with structure. The liberation of the legislature—and the restoration of lawmaking independence from party machinery—is the essential first step toward dismantling elite dominance. Only a truly representative and autonomous legislative body can begin to reverse the institutional capture that has accumulated over decades.

Some may argue that the core problem lies in the economic system itself—whether in the workings of markets, the nature of capital accumulation, or the structure of global finance. These are valid concerns. Yet no meaningful economic reform, of any kind, can take place while the lawmaking process remains under elite control. Before capitalism or socialism—or any alternative—can be meaningfully debated, the terms of that debate must be reclaimed.

Party systems do not merely distort democracy; they facilitate the quiet and methodical conquest of the state by entrenched interests. Reversing that capture must begin where power is codified—in the legislature. A chamber composed of independently elected representatives is not an idealistic abstraction; it is the minimal condition for genuine democratic function.

Of course, any representative chamber will reflect the diversity and imperfections of the society it serves. Some elected individuals may act out of self-interest; others may hold radical or unorthodox views. But these are exceptions, not the norm. In practice, most candidates—in order to gain the trust of a broad and diverse electorate—are compelled to offer platforms that are moderate, inclusive, and grounded in practical realities.

While segments of the public may hold extreme views, the individuals they elect are, by necessity, those who are more likely to be educated, capable of engaging with complexity, communicating across divides, and navigating competing priorities. Representatives are expected to digest policy detail, weigh evidence, and build consensus—functions that naturally reward competence over provocation. The result is a deliberative assembly shaped by public reasoning rather than elite command—one where the professional demands of governance tend to temper ideological extremes.

Modern elections are not contests of ideas—they are filtered menus. You do not get to choose who runs. You choose from those already chosen.

In the United States, the gate is guarded by primaries—not open debates, but internal trials of loyalty. In closed primary states, independents—nearly half the electorate—are barred from participating. Candidates must first survive this insider crucible, where success means winning the favour of donors, party bosses, and media gatekeepers.

Ask Bernie Sanders what happens when you dare to run outside the script. Twice, he ignited a movement of millions—teachers, veterans, single mothers, young workers—who rallied behind a vision of justice, healthcare, and corporate accountability. Twice, the Democratic Party pulled the rug out. In 2016, leaked emails exposed how the party worked behind the scenes to tip the scale for Hillary Clinton. In 2020, a sudden orchestration of endorsements cleared the path for Joe Biden—just days before Super Tuesday—to halt Sanders' momentum.

In the U.K., Jeremy Corbyn, propelled to leadership by a surge of grassroots enthusiasm, was met with relentless sabotage from within his own ranks. MPs plotted against him. Donors deserted him. The media painted him as dangerous. And after Labour's 2019 defeat, rule changes were introduced to prevent anyone like him from ever rising again.

Even sitting MPs aren't safe.

Diane Abbott, the first Black woman elected to Parliament, was suspended from the Labour Party in 2023 after a controversial letter—despite issuing a full apology and completing training. She was later reinstated, and in May 2024, reports suggested she might be barred from standing in the general election. After public backlash, Keir Starmer said she was free to run—and she did. In July 2025, she was suspended again over separate comments, fuelling accusations of a quiet purge, a "cull of leftwingers" designed to sanitise the party.

Under Boris Johnson, the Conservative Party expelled 21 MPs—including former Chancellors—simply for voting against a no-deal Brexit.

In a true democracy, the people decide who speaks for them. In the current system, candidates must pass a loyalty test—not to voters, but to party orthodoxy. If your views challenge war profiteers, financial elites, or donor interests, you are simply removed from the menu.

Democracy begins with free access. And where access is filtered, democracy is fiction. Even if you manage to climb through the gauntlet, win the vote, and earn your seat—your freedom doesn't begin. It ends.

Because once you're inside the halls of power, the party tightens its grip. You don't speak for your constituents anymore. You speak for the whip.

In the U.K., the party whip system operates like a hammer. Members of Parliament are told how to vote—not advised, told. If they disobey, they're deselected, sidelined, or quietly destroyed. The whip isn't just a suggestion. It's a leash.

Remember the lead-up to the Iraq War in 2003? Millions marched in the streets. The public screamed "No." But inside Parliament, MPs lined up like soldiers—whipped into submission. Both Labour and Conservative members voted for a war built on lies. Not because they believed in it, but because the party told them to.

In the United States, the whip may not wear a title, but its presence is no less suffocating. Here, obedience is enforced through money, media, and access. Step out of line, and the donors vanish. The cameras disappear. Your future evaporates.

Votes are traded like currency. Lobbyists draft the laws. Party bosses decide the agenda. And representatives become little more than placeholders—filling seats, pressing buttons, reciting scripts.

In the modern political marketplace, money is the gatekeeper. It decides who gets airtime, who gets staff, who gets on the debate stage—and who gets erased. Parties don't just organise candidates; they act as financial gatekeepers, funnelling wealth from mega-donors, corporations, and political action committees into campaigns that promise one thing: to protect the system that feeds them.

As political scientist Martin Gilens has shown in landmark research, U.S. policy overwhelmingly reflects the preferences of the wealthy. The general public's opinions? Statistically irrelevant. In other words: if you don't have money, you don't have power—not even a voice.

In the U.K., the rot runs just as deep. Party conferences are sponsored by banks, oil companies, and arms manufacturers. Ministers meet with hedge fund managers more often than food bank volunteers. The message is clear: pay to play—or stay silent.

In a No-Party democracy, this dynamic breaks. Without centralised party funding, no donor can buy access to an entire bloc of candidates. Every representative must earn trust locally. Every campaign must declare its finances in real time. And with equal public funding and strict donation limits, the size of your wallet no longer determines the reach of your voice.

It's not perfect. But it is fairer—and infinitely more honest.

Chapter 10

Political Religion

Worshipping the Party as a Way of Life

THE GREATEST TRIUMPH of modern power is not forcing obedience at gunpoint but convincing the public that obedience is freedom.

Political parties have dressed themselves in the noble garments of democracy. They claimed to be the voice of the people—conduits for collective will, defenders of the common good. History books echo their tale like gospel, repeating the myth that parties arose to give us power, to organise our chaos into meaningful choice.

But peel back the veneer, and a darker truth emerges.

Political parties were not created to expand our agency. They were created to discipline it. From their earliest days in the parliaments of Britain and the town halls of America, parties functioned less as megaphones for the people and more as cages for dissent. Their true mission wasn't to liberate voices—it was to corral them. To filter, to tame, to pre-select which cries for change would be heard, and which would be drowned in silence.

They didn't throw open the gates of democracy—they built checkpoints. They didn't invite free debate—they orchestrated controlled duels. And at every step, they ensured that the spoils of governance remained in the hands of the already powerful.

Yes, the system evolved. But the formula stayed the same:

- **Let the people feel heard, but never let them speak beyond the script.**
- **Offer the illusion of control, while tightening the grip behind the curtain.**
- **Replace loyalty to ideas with loyalty to institutions.**

This is the paradox of modern democracy: a system that demands devotion, yet offers only stagecraft in return. A structure that calls us free, while binding us to choices crafted in backrooms long before the first vote is cast.

Political parties, guided by the interests that fund and shape them, have mastered a subtler form of control—not through force, but through ritual. Elections ceased to be decisions. They became performances. Not levers of power, but stages for collective catharsis. The vote—once a radical tool of self-governance—has been transfigured into a kind of national sacrament. You don't just vote. You participate. You fulfil your duty. You're told that marking a pre-approved name on a ballot is the pinnacle of freedom—even when that name was chosen for you by money, media, and machinery you'll never see.

The act becomes holy. And like all holy rituals, it delivers emotional absolution:

- **You feel powerful for a day, even if your conditions remain unchanged.**
- **You're told your voice was heard, even if the outcome was predetermined.**
- **You experience unity, patriotism, purpose—even as the system marches on without you.**

Voting becomes less a mechanism of control over government and more a sedative. A pressure valve. A symbolic nod that distracts you from asking the real questions:

- Who chose these candidates?
- Why do they all seem to serve the same interests?
- What happens when neither option represents you?

You are encouraged to *feel* like a citizen, not *be* one. To express emotion, not exert power. To shout in the streets or cry at rallies—then return to silence until the next cycle. You vote. You hope. You despair. And then, you wait. You have not chosen your destiny. You have simply played your part.

To rule effectively, power must move from the whip to the soul. And so, the parties didn't just demand your loyalty—they made you believe it was who you are. Obedience became a virtue. Allegiance, a moral badge. Support for your party wasn't just political preference—it was a measure of your decency, your values, your *very self*.

Behind the scenes, elite-funded think tanks and behavioural specialists mapped the architecture of belief. They didn't want to win debates—they wanted to win identities. To weave party loyalty so deeply into your psyche that questioning it would feel like questioning your own worth.

And it worked.

No longer were citizens independent minds assessing competing ideas. They became tribal soldiers, pledging fealty to colours, flags, and slogans. Politics was reframed as sport. Pick a team. Wear the badge. Cheer for your side—no matter how badly it plays.

It didn't matter if both sides served the same masters. It didn't matter if the policies were nearly identical behind the rhetoric. What mattered was the *fight*. The rivalry. The sense of belonging. Being a "good citizen" now meant being a *faithful* one:

- Faithful to your party, no matter the scandals.
- Faithful to your leader, no matter the betrayals.
- Faithful to the system, no matter how little it gave you in return.

To anchor this identity, parties flooded the culture with symbols designed to bypass thought:

- Logos, colours, and flags.
- Slogans that wrap complexity in candy-coated simplicity: "Hope and Change." "Take Back Control." "Stronger Together." "Make America Great Again." "Build the Wall." "Drain the Swamp."
- Rallies, conventions, national anthems—all orchestrated to make partisanship feel like patriotism.

The true genius of the party system is not that it demands obedience—but that it gets citizens to *enforce it themselves*. Once party loyalty becomes identity, the state no longer needs censors or enforcers. The people do the job for them.

- Speak out against the system? You'll be ridiculed by your neighbours.
- Suggest that elections are a managed illusion? You'll be dismissed as a crank.
- Propose a world without parties? You'll be labelled extreme, unpatriotic, or dangerous.

Citizens become the prison guards of their own political consciousness. They defend the very structures that betray them. They attack those who question the legitimacy of rigged processes. They mock those brave enough to say, "This is not real democracy." This is the final triumph of the party system:

- It transforms obedience into pride.
- It transforms conformity into honour.
- It transforms disempowerment into participation.

The result is a society where:

- Citizens cling to their parties as lifeboats—even when the ship is sinking.
- They confuse defending a faction with defending freedom.
- They shut their eyes to alternatives before even looking.

The system does not need to hide its betrayals. Because the betrayed have been trained to love their chains. Once emotional loyalty is secured, it becomes a powerful shield—one that protects the ruling elite from scrutiny, even as they strip the people of power.

Citizens, loyal to their chosen faction, come to believe that their side is the path to salvation … while the other is the path to ruin. They invest their hopes, fears, and identities into electoral contests that feel like epic battles—but in truth, are shadow plays. Costumes change. The script does not.

And beneath the drama, the same interests stay seated at the throne. This is the dark magic of engineered obedience: People give their consent to systems that subjugate them—not through fear, but through emotional investment in a story that was never theirs. No matter who wins, the pillars of elite rule remain untouched.

- Economic Policy: The markets stay happy. Deregulation continues. Corporate subsidies remain sacred. Billionaires are bailed out; the public is told to tighten its belt.
- Foreign Policy: Interventionism, arms deals, and military alliances with oppressive regimes endure—no matter which party waves the flag.
- Surveillance and Security: The machinery of control grows. Cameras multiply. Civil liberties shrink. Privacy becomes a relic.
- Social Inequality: The rich grow richer. The poor are pacified with crumbs. Redistribution is discussed, never done.

Parties bicker over budgets and slogans while marching in lockstep toward the same destination: sustained elite dominance. And still, citizens cheer. Because they've been trained not to see reality—but to see *teams*.

- When their party betrays them, they excuse it.
- When the other party does the same, they roar in outrage.
- They accept crumbs as revolutions and symbols as substance.

For all its confidence, all its pageantry, all its ritualised manipulation—the party system is built on sand. It doesn't fear scandals. It doesn't fear economic collapse. It doesn't fear war, fraud, or public outrage.

It fears one thing only: awakening. Not the fleeting kind that comes with a broken promise or a bad leader—those are easily absorbed by the machine. No, the true threat is the moment when citizens realise:

- That betrayal isn't an accident—it's *the design*.
- That both parties serve the same masters.
- That choosing between elite-approved options is not freedom, but theatre.
- That real democracy would mean breaking the script altogether.

The Moment of Awakening

It is not born of scandal or shame. It is born of clarity. The moment when a citizen no longer says, *"We need better leaders,"* but instead asks, *"Why do we let these institutions rule at all?"*

It is the moment when obedience becomes absurd. When slogans lose their spell. When rituals feel hollow. When the citizen no longer yearns to *belong*, but to *be free*. And that, above all, terrifies the architects of the party state. Because awakened citizens:

- **Do not plead for reform.**
- **They do not beg for better managers.**
- **They *walk away* from the system itself.**

The party system can survive almost anything—except the people it claims to serve finally standing up and saying: *We see you.*

It can survive:

- **Sex scandals.**
- **Economic meltdowns.**
- **Foreign wars and mass protests.**

But it cannot survive a mass awakening of independent, self-governing citizens who no longer ask permission to be free. It cannot survive people who:

- **Reject tribalism.**
- **Stop clinging to brands.**
- **Stop choosing between pre-selected evils.**

These people are not dangerous because they riot. They are dangerous because they *refuse to be managed*. They do not want to switch brands. They want to smash the shelf. They want to write new rules, build new structures, and reclaim what was always theirs—sovereignty. And that's what terrifies the system. Because independent citizens:

- **Can't be herded.**
- **Can't be guilt-tripped.**
- **Can't be hypnotised by flags, colours, or slogans.**

They do not see themselves as *consumers of politics*. They see themselves as *authors of democracy*. And once they awaken, they don't just leave the game. They expose the whole thing as a con.

Every journey toward freedom begins with a moment of reckoning. And the first step is the hardest: *to see clearly*. To see that your loyalty has been weaponised. To see that the system was never broken—it was *built* this way. To see that the rituals you were taught to revere were never yours to begin with.

It is painful. It requires shedding comforting myths:

- That "your" party is the lesser evil.
- That change comes slowly, if you're patient.
- That democracy means choosing between pre-approved elites.

In modern party democracies, allegiance is no longer rooted in values, ideas, or policy outcomes. Instead, it is emotional, visceral, and often irrational. For millions of voters, their connection to a political party and its leader mirrors the intensity of religious faith or tribal loyalty. This is not democratic engagement; it is identity politics at its most dangerous, where political affiliation becomes a form of spiritual warfare, and elections are perceived as matters of existential dread.

What sustains this dynamic is not merely a clash of policies, but the very structure of the party system. It transforms political disagreement into identity warfare. Fear of the opposing party doesn't just motivate voters; it radicalises them. Loyalty is no longer based on belief in one's own side but in hostility toward the other. Voters no longer choose policies; they vote to prevent their perceived enemies from winning. With each election cycle, supporters grow more entrenched, emotionally bound to their party, and resistant to reason. The party becomes a shield, the opposition a threat, and democracy a zero-sum game of survival.

Without parties as official entities on the ballot, in the media, or in the legislature, the emotional infrastructure that binds voters through fear begins to dissolve.

In Democracy for Realists, political scientists Christopher H. Achen and Larry M. Bartels challenge the traditional folk theory of democracy—the idea that citizens vote as well-informed, independent decision-makers. Instead, they argue, most people vote based on deep-seated partisan loyalties rather than reasoned evaluation. This makes the system vulnerable to manipulation by powerful interest groups, eroding the democratic ideal.

According to Achen and Bartels, the vision of the sovereign, rational voter—celebrated by thinkers like Robert Dahl and Walt Whitman—is more myth than reality. In practice, most citizens are consumed by the demands of daily life: work, family, and personal obligations. They simply lack the time and capacity to engage with politics as the idealized model of democracy expects. As a result, voting behavior is shaped less by reason and more by social identity. People align with parties that reflect their cultural or community affiliations—even when those parties no longer serve their actual interests. Loyalty to political "tribes" becomes emotional and habitual.

This is not just a personal failing; it is a structural one. For over a century, the education system—shaped by industrial-era figures like Henry Ford and Andrew Carnegie—has trained citizens not to question authority, but to obey it. Designed to serve hierarchical systems, it discourages critical thought and encourages conformity. This legacy benefits entrenched elites who rely on a compliant electorate: voters who comply rather than critique, who follow rather than question.

In this context, the party system plays a central role. It thrives on conflict, false choices, and inherited allegiance. Entire towns or regions vote the same way for generations, not because of policy but because of identity—shaped by party myths and generational loyalty. The result is a system of organized hostility, where disagreement is less about ideas and more about tribal allegiance.

In a No-Party system, candidates must earn trust directly from the people they seek to represent. They cannot lean on partisan branding or inherited loyalty; they must build support through personal integrity, policy merit, and demonstrated commitment to the public good.

This structure introduces an additional safeguard—one rooted in how people already make decisions in complex areas of life. Just as citizens choose lawyers, doctors, or financial advisors based on available information and personal trust, local representatives in a No-Party democracy can play a similar role. Voters do not need to become policy experts themselves; they need only choose individuals they believe will represent their interests faithfully and effectively. And, crucially, they can replace those representatives when they no longer deliver. In a world where, as Achen and Bartels argue, well-informed, fully rational voters are the exception, this system of choosing individual representatives—rather than parties—offers a practical, functional mechanism for political accountability.

This does not eliminate political disagreement—nor should it. Debate and dissent are essential to any functioning democracy. But removing the party structure dismantles the machinery that mass-produces political identity through fear and division. Without party banners to rally behind, blind allegiance becomes harder to sustain. Accountability becomes easier to demand. The emotional temperature of politics cools. Disagreement still exists, but it no longer has to escalate into hatred.

This structural reform isn't a silver bullet. Removing the party structure isn't a cure-all—it won't eliminate ignorance, conformity, or emotionally driven behaviour. Some citizens will always follow headlines, peer groups, or influencers without critical reflection. But it disrupts the engineered cycle where fear fuels loyalty, and loyalty demands more fear. By dismantling the machinery that mass-produces partisan identity, we create space for a different kind of political culture to emerge. Combined with reforms in education, independent media, and civic institutions, the long-term effect could be a more thoughtful, engaged electorate. It may take generations, but it moves us in the right direction.

The ancient Roman strategy of "bread and circuses"—offering food and entertainment to distract the masses from political decline—finds a modern echo in today's media-saturated, economically strained societies. Political and economic elites benefit from, and often perpetuate, a system in which citizens are immersed in constant entertainment—from sports and streaming platforms to digital games—that provides instant gratification while diverting attention from deeper structural issues. At the same time, public resources are funnelled into foreign aid packages, regime change efforts, and endless wars that cost billions, often with little transparency or clear benefit to the public. Meanwhile, economic insecurity at home—through stagnant wages, rising living costs, and a fraying social safety net—keeps much of the population preoccupied with survival.

An ignorant citizen, in this context, is not a flaw in the system—it is the system's greatest achievement. While we are told that democracy depends on an informed public, this ideal is quietly inverted under the rule of permanent political parties. These systems don't require citizens who understand; they require citizens who obey—people who feel smart enough to vote, but not wise enough to question what they're voting for. They are trained to participate in political rituals, but not to interrogate the machinery that writes the script. Viewed through the lens of Maslow's hierarchy of needs, this environment traps citizens at the lower levels of existence, leaving them politically passive. In such a world, disengagement is not just tolerated; it is cultivated, ensuring that power remains unchallenged and comfortably entrenched.

This isn't negligence. It's strategy. Because once people begin to think in structural terms—once they start seeing the architecture of control—the party system becomes ungovernable. So ignorance must be manufactured. Not with silence, but with noise. Not by withholding information, but by overwhelming it with triviality. Not by suppressing education, but by warping it—so that obedience looks like wisdom.

The ideal citizen for party rule is not a blank slate. It's someone emotionally engaged but intellectually confined.

- A person who votes passionately, but never reads a policy draft.
- A person who loves their party, but couldn't explain the lobbying laws that shape its actions.
- A person who believes they're informed—because they consume headlines, not history.

This kind of consciousness is perfect for maintaining the illusion of democracy:

- High voter turnout, low systemic understanding.
- Loud debates, empty substance.
- Endless outrage, no rebellion.

The system is designed to keep citizens in a state of emotional intensity, without ever pushing them to truly engage or critically reflect on the structure itself. By fostering a public that confuses noise with action, and passion with reason, the party system ensures the status quo remains unchallenged, even as it thrives on superficial engagement.

If political parties thrive on shallow political awareness, schools become their first factories of consent. From the first bell to the last exam, children are not raised to be sovereign citizens; they are trained to fit in, to respect authority, to memorise rituals, and to follow systems they're never invited to question. They are told that democracy is sacred, but never told how it's been bought. They are taught to vote, but not to investigate who funds the candidates, writes the laws, or shapes the debates. They learn the rules of the game, but not who wrote the rulebook.

Public schooling was never designed to empower free thinkers—it arose to meet the needs of an industrial order. It trained factory workers, not philosophers; employees, not dissidents. Concepts like punctuality, obedience, and standardisation were embedded to prepare students for clockwork labour, acceptance of authority, and conformity. Civics education followed the same path, teaching students to celebrate the vote and institutions without questioning the machinery behind them. They memorised the names of leaders but never explored the flow of power.

Civics, in its current form, is a containment strategy. It instructs people on what to do—vote, campaign, respect institutions—but never how party financing captures policy, how both major parties often serve elite consensus, or how governance might look without party lines. By the time students reach voting age, the central lie is already embedded in their thinking: democracy means choosing between parties, and questioning this is irrational or dangerous.

Thus, schools don't fail democracy. They are designed to produce the exact kind of citizen the system needs: loyal, emotionally driven, partially informed, and easily managed.

If schools lay the foundation for engineered ignorance, the media system builds the walls and locks the doors. In an ideal democracy, the media would shine a light into dark corners, expose corruption, and elevate unheard voices. Instead, under party rule, the media reflects only what the powerful want you to see. It doesn't question power; it manages perception. It narrows understanding, leaving only the illusion of choice.

Most major media outlets are not independent arbiters of truth. They are influenced by the same elite networks that finance political campaigns and shape party agendas. This results in a narrow debate, with structural critiques excluded, elections framed as personality contests, and the public herded into ideological pens—left vs. right, us vs. them. Meanwhile, the corporate masters pulling the strings remain untouched. The media reinforces this system emotionally: celebrating "your team," demonising the other, and distracting from the fact that both parties operate within the same corrupted architecture.

In this media landscape, questioning the system is not engaged with—it is erased. Raise doubts about party capture, and you're labelled "unrealistic." Challenge the role of money in elections, and you're "radical." Speak of democracy without permanent parties, and you're "conspiratorial" or "extremist." The boundaries are clear:

you may argue within the party framework, but you may never challenge the necessity of that framework itself.

If reality alone could awaken people, the party system would have crumbled long ago. We've lived through scandal after scandal, financial collapse, endless wars, and betrayals so blatant they leave blood on the floors of Parliament and Capitol Hill alike. And yet, the system endures. Not because people are apathetic, but because they are loyal—loyal to a story that has been stitched into their very identity.

When political loyalty becomes personal identity, it's no longer just about supporting a party; it's about defending yourself. When your party fails, you rationalise it. When the other party fails, you weaponise it. When both fail, you retreat into fear: "At least mine is better." Admitting that both parties are rigged, both serve elite interests, and both are illusions would mean admitting that your loyalty was misplaced, that your efforts were hijacked, that your participation served to contain you. For many, that pain is too much to bear. So they double down, argue harder, wear their colours more proudly, and invest more energy into a machine that has already proven it doesn't work for them.

The party system understands this. Every disaster becomes an opportunity for deeper control. An economic crash becomes a chance to blame the other party's spending or cuts. A failed war is an opportunity to blame the strategy, not the bipartisan hunger for empire. A broken healthcare system is a chance to point fingers at the enemy for underfunding or overspending. Every structural failure becomes a partisan football, never a moment to question the stadium itself. The conversation never changes: Who messed up? Which party botched it? Who should we punish next election? It's never about why we continue entrusting corrupt institutions with our futures or what it would mean to break the system open. Even in collapse, the party system thrives because it has trained us to look at each other—not above.

Perhaps the most seductive lie of the party system is the idea that change takes time. You're told that progress is slow but sure, that if you just elect better people—smarter, kinder, more ethical—things will improve. That if you stay loyal, stay hopeful, stay in line, reform will come. But the truth is this: the system isn't slow because it's careful. It's slow because it's designed never to arrive.

This myth keeps you walking in circles, chasing carrots hung on sticks by men who never intended to feed you. You want justice? Wait for the next election. You want peace? Support this war to stop the next one. You want change? Donate, volunteer, canvas—so the party can disappoint you more efficiently next time. Every cycle becomes a new hope. Every betrayal becomes a lesson in patience. Every outrage becomes an opportunity to double down on a system that continues to betray its promises.

By clinging to the idea that the system will eventually deliver, citizens forgive the unforgivable, accept symbolic reforms as real change, and condemn those who demand structural transformation as "unrealistic." And so, the machine lurches forward, repainting its face every few years, but never altering its spine. Meanwhile, inequality deepens, climate collapse accelerates, war machines keep spinning, surveillance expands, and corporate power takes root so deep, no election can uproot it. And still, people chant: "Next time. The next leader. The next bill. The next turn of the wheel." This is not hope. It is a cultivated paralysis.

If ignorance is the soil in which party systems grow, then critical education is the wildfire that could burn the whole plantation down. And that's why it is so aggressively contained. No reform within the current framework—no new curriculum, no civic awareness campaign, no media watchdog—can fix the root problem. The rot is the structure itself. As long as permanent political parties control the levers of governance, ignorance will remain the norm—not because the public is lazy, but because the system needs them to remain docile. It needs loyalty without scrutiny, emotion without understanding, and participation without comprehension. It survives by suppressing awakening. The only true antidote is the destruction of the very structure that engineers obedience—the complete removal of party dominance from political life.

The difference between a partisan system and a No-Party democracy is not merely mechanical; it is fundamentally a question of human dignity and autonomy. The partisan system does not simply manipulate the mechanics of governance—it manipulates the very consciousness of the people, shaping how they understand their role in society and the power they wield, or fail to wield, within it.

In a partisan system:

- Politics becomes a spectacle, not a meaningful engagement with public life.
- Loyalty is demanded, but it is loyalty to a party, not to principle or truth.
- Education serves not to enlighten, but to reinforce a narrow, controlled narrative.
- Citizenship is reduced to a passive, consumer-like transaction, where participation is limited to voting every few years, without genuine power or responsibility.

But in a No-Party democracy, the shift is profound:

- Engagement is continuous—there is no "off-season" for democracy.
- Accountability is direct and unmediated by party structures, ensuring that those in power are genuinely accountable to the people.
- Representation is earned by each individual, rooted in their personal integrity and commitment to the public good.
- Education is not a tool for indoctrination, but a critical, ongoing process of inquiry and participation, central to the preservation of liberty.

In such a system, critical thinking would not be viewed as a threat, but as an essential part of democratic life. Awareness would not be stifled, but actively cultivated as a necessary condition for self-governance. Citizens would no longer be herded into ideological silos; they would be empowered to participate in the shaping of their society.

This is not the promise of a perfect society—it is the promise of a society where the people are free to determine their own future. Real democracy is not a ritual to be performed every few years, nor is it a spectacle for public consumption. It is the ongoing, living practice of self-rule, where the people themselves are the authors of their collective destiny.

And it begins not with the question, "Which party will save us?" but with a much more radical question: "Why do we need parties at all?"

Until We Dismantle the Party System:

- **Ignorance will remain the primary tool of control.**
- **Loyalty will continue to be mistaken for virtue, and critical thought will be branded as subversive.**
- **Freedom will continue to be a performance, staged by the very elites who profit from its illusion.**

But the moment we awaken—the moment we see clearly—the system's false promises fall away. We will remember what was stolen from us: our agency, our voice, and our power. And in that moment, we will begin to take it back. Not as passive subjects, but as free citizens reclaiming their birthright.

Chapter 11

Democracy Is a Journey, Not a Destination

*From Parties to People:
The Next Step in Democratic Evolution*

We are taught from childhood that we live in a democracy—that our governments operate with the consent of the governed, that our vote is our voice, and that the people hold the power. This idea is repeated so often, in schools and speeches and news reports, that it begins to feel sacred. Untouchable.

But stop and ask yourself: **when was the last time the will of the people actually shaped policy?** Not slogans. Not speeches. Not symbolic gestures. Real decisions. Real power.

We are told democracy is rule by the people. But for most of its history—and still today—it has been **rule over the people**, dressed up in the language of liberty.

To understand how this came to be, we must trace democracy back to its origins—and follow its long, bitter path of exclusion, co-optation, and control. Because while its form has evolved, its function has remained disturbingly consistent: **to keep real power out of the hands of the many and tightly held by the few.**

The word "democracy" comes from the Greek *demos* (people) and *kratos* (power). But in 5th-century BCE Athens—the birthplace of the idea—"the people" did not mean everyone. Democracy in Athens was revolutionary—but only for a few. Only property-owning male citizens had a voice. Women, the poor, and the dispossessed were locked out entirely. The idea of rule by "the people" was born—but "the people" was a tiny, protected class.

Yes, Athenian democracy was revolutionary for its time. But it was also brutally elitist. It wasn't designed to empower the masses—it was designed to prevent total monarchy by letting a small class of citizens negotiate amongst themselves.

The Roman Republic refined the model—introducing a more layered system with senates, assemblies, and magistrates. But this, too, was a balancing act among elites. The Senate, supposedly the voice of reason and order, was a playground for aristocrats. Corruption, patronage, and backdoor influence were not bugs of the system—they were how the system ran.

When Rome fell, Europe descended into the cold grip of feudalism. Kings ruled by divine right. Power passed through bloodlines, not ballots. The idea of representation became a distant dream—and would remain so for centuries.

The seeds of modern democracy were sown in revolt—not gifted by the powerful, but wrestled from them. In 1215, England's Magna Carta forced the king to accept that even monarchs were not above the law—though its protections only extended to nobles. Still, it was the beginning of a crack in the old world order.

By the 17th and 18th centuries, Enlightenment thinkers were lighting intellectual fires across Europe. **John Locke** spoke of natural rights. **Montesquieu** of checks and balances. **Rousseau** of the social contract. They imagined a world where people governed themselves, not through inherited privilege or divine rule, but through **consent**.

These were not harmless ideas. They were dynamite. They fuelled the American Revolution in 1776 and the French Revolution in 1789. Both overthrew monarchies in the name of liberty, equality, and popular sovereignty.

But even these revolutions—often mythologised as triumphs of democracy—were riddled with hypocrisy. The American founding fathers wrote of freedom while enslaving human beings. The Constitution was drafted by white, land-owning men—and protected the power of their class. Women were silenced. Native Americans were erased. The poor were locked out. The French, after declaring universal rights, spiralled into chaos and eventually installed Napoleon—trading kings for emperors while exporting revolutionary rhetoric abroad.

It wasn't until the Industrial Revolution that the democratic experiment truly began to expand—and even then, only when the ruling class had no choice. As factories replaced farms and workers flooded into cities, the new capitalist elite faced growing pressure from an increasingly organised working class. Reforms came slowly, reluctantly, and only under sustained mobilisation, protest, and the looming threat of revolt.

In the UK, the right to vote was never freely given—it was prised open over centuries of struggle. The first men were granted voting rights in 1432, limited to wealthy landowners. Over time, the electorate slowly widened through the Reform Acts of 1832, 1867, and 1884—each step reluctantly conceded under pressure. Universal male suffrage did not arrive until 1918, when all men over 21 were finally enfranchised.

Women, by contrast, were shut out entirely for nearly five centuries. It was not until 1918 that women over 30, and only those meeting property requirements, were granted the vote. Full equal voting rights—the same as men—did not come until 1928. That's 496 years after the first men cast ballots.

In the U.S., the story is no less damning. The franchise began with white male landowners. Black men were legally granted the vote in 1870, but across the South, voter suppression, lynching, and Jim Crow laws rendered that right largely meaningless for another century. Women gained the vote in 1920—a staggering 144 years after the Declaration of Independence. Indigenous Americans were only guaranteed voting rights in 1965, and even then, many barriers remained. The Voting Rights Act of 1965 was not a gift. It was earned through blood, beatings, marches, and martyrdom.

This delayed inclusion isn't unique to the U.S. or UK—it's a global pattern:

- **France: Women were barred from voting until 1944—155 years after the French Revolution began.**
- **Switzerland: Long seen as a beacon of neutrality, it denied federal voting rights to women until 1971—over a century after universal male suffrage (1848). Some cantons resisted until 1991.**
- **Canada: Indigenous peoples were excluded from federal voting unless they renounced treaty rights until 1960—over 90 years after non-Indigenous men.**
- **Australia: Aboriginal Australians were not granted full voting rights until 1962—more than 60 years after white men, and nearly 160 years after colonisation began.**

These are not footnotes. They are the central story of modern democracy: A system never designed to be inclusive—only made so through relentless pressure from below.

The American Founding Fathers warned of it—the rise of factions, the decay of representation, the slow death of democracy under the weight of organised power. Their warnings were not outdated relics. They were prophecies.

Because democracy is not a finished product. It's not something you achieve, install, and forget. It's a battlefield. And in most of the world today—including the so-called democratic West—it's a lost one.

In autocratic states like Russia, Iran, or China, the performance of democracy is staged with brutal efficiency. They have parliaments. They have ballots. They use the language of the people. But it's a lie.

Opposition candidates are jailed or disqualified. Journalists are silenced. Media is controlled. Every institution is wired to preserve a single truth: power does not change hands unless the powerful allow it.

In Russia, "elections" are held while dissenters are exiled, poisoned, or imprisoned. In Iran, candidates must be approved by religious authorities—the people may vote, but only from a list of the pre-cleansed. In China, local voting exists—but the Communist Party answers to no one. The illusion of choice is just enough to prevent revolt. These are not democracies. They are control systems disguised as consent. The outward symbols exist not to empower, but to pacify. Participation is permitted—as long as it changes nothing.

Western democracies wear different masks—but the game is eerily similar. In the United States, citizens are told they live in the greatest democracy on Earth. But look closer. It is a system locked into a two-party stranglehold, where both parties are funded by the same industries, advised by the same consultants, and protected by the same media networks.

The people "vote"—but the field has already been cleared, narrowed, sanitised. This isn't a democracy. It's a well-rehearsed performance. The public is handed a script and told it's power. In place of bans and brute force, Western democracies rely on:

- **Narrative management**
- **Manufactured outrage**
- **Carefully engineered debates**
- **Emotional distraction**
- **And a revolving cast of politicians that differ in tone, but not in allegiance**

Where authoritarian regimes crush dissent with violence, Western democracies neutralise it with ritual. They offer commissions, panels, and symbolic gestures. They appoint watchdogs that bark but never bite. They host debates where no real alternatives are allowed on stage. Elections are held. Promises are made. But the core power structures—the financial interests, the party hierarchies, the corporate lobbies—remain untouched.

We're told that the West has reached the endpoint of democratic development—that with regular elections and constitutional safeguards, the mission is complete. But this is a lie told by the comfortable to the complacent. Democracy has never been static. It has always been a fight—and always against the same enemy: concentrated power. Every expansion of rights, every act of inclusion—from suffrage to civil rights—was met with resistance. Nothing was granted. Everything was fought for. And everything can be taken back.

The idea that democracy only moves forward is not hope—it's delusion. You're told you live in a free society. That your vote counts. That you have a voice. But ask yourself:

- **If the same billionaires fund both major parties, what are you really choosing?**
- **If lobbyists write the laws, what is your representative really representing?**
- **If the media decides who is "viable," who is deciding your future?**
- **If dissent is permitted only when harmless, is it really dissent?**

For too long, we've been told that political parties are the lifeblood of democracy—that without them, democracy would wither and die. But what if that belief is a myth? What if, far from sustaining democratic life, parties have become the very chains that bind it?

The belief in political parties as sacred institutions has been so deeply drilled into the public consciousness that questioning their role feels like sacrilege. Yet neither history nor reason supports their sanctity. Political parties were not delivered on stone tablets from democratic gods—they were invented, improvised, and imposed by those seeking to navigate the messiness of power. To equate democracy with partisan politics is like confusing the scaffolding with the building itself. It's not just mistaken; it's dangerous.

Democracy is not a trophy to be won and displayed in a glass case. It is a living, breathing struggle—a journey without end, always striving toward more justice, more participation, more dignity for all. And if democracy truly is a journey, then we must admit that we've taken a wrong turn. Because the political systems that dominate today are not moving us forward.

If democracy were a destination, then modern party systems are the tollbooths, gatekeeping who may pass and under what terms. But if we are honest, these tollbooths do not serve the people. Political parties, in their modern form, are not engines of democracy. They are its detours—rerouting power away from the people and into the hands of those who've learned to manipulate the system for their own ends.

So why do we remain loyal to the very institutions that have betrayed us? Why do we cling to the fiction that partisanship is synonymous with democracy when the evidence screams otherwise? It is time to cast off this illusion—to see parties not as inevitable, but as optional. Not as the final stage of democratic evolution, but as a phase we must now outgrow.

A No-Party democracy is a necessary correction. A course adjustment. The next, most logical step forward on democracy's long and unfinished journey.

Political Parties Are a Historical Accident, Not a Divine Mandate

Imagine mistaking a crutch for a leg—and then being told you can't walk without it. That's how deeply embedded the myth of political parties has become. We are told they are the skeleton of democracy, when in truth, they are prosthetics—artificial limbs strapped onto systems that could, with time and care, learn to stand on their own.

The rise of political parties wasn't the result of noble democratic engineering. It wasn't the outcome of some great philosophical consensus. It was a scramble—a messy, improvised response to the challenges of power, conflict, and scale. In Athens, the birthplace of democracy, no parties existed. Citizens spoke and voted as themselves, not as mouthpieces of factions. Democracy meant showing up, not signing up.

When the architects of the American republic debated the future of self-governance, their warnings rang like fire alarms. George Washington, in his Farewell Address, didn't merely criticise parties—he feared them. He saw in them "potent engines" for manipulation, division, and betrayal. Madison and Jefferson, too, wrestled with the corrosive nature of factionalism. They knew that once loyalty to a faction overtook loyalty to the public good, democracy would become a theatre—a carefully managed illusion.

And yet, the gravitational pull of faction was too strong to resist. Organising votes required alliances. Winning power required machinery. Parties emerged—not out of democratic triumph, but out of political expediency. What began as temporary teams hardened into permanent machines. And like any machine built to capture power, they soon learned how to keep it.

From that moment on, the history of democracy has been shackled to a paradox: parties, originally created to navigate power, evolved into institutions that hoard it. They gatekeep who can run. They script the debates. They rig the rules. They narrow the terms of public conversation to a safe and sterile bandwidth.

To continue believing that democracy and political parties are inseparable is to forget that democracy came first—and thrived longest when it belonged directly to the people. Parties are not divine mandates. They are political habits—bad ones—that have grown so familiar we mistake them for necessity.

Democracy as an Evolving Ideal

From its very beginnings, democracy has been a work in progress—not a pristine artefact but a hard-fought rebellion against exclusion and control. The Athenian model, so often romanticised, was in truth a democracy for the few. Women were silenced. Slaves were owned. Foreigners were disregarded. It was a circle of participation drawn tightly around a privileged elite—a prototype, not a promise fulfilled.

The same is true of early America. Its founding myths speak of liberty and representation, but its reality was one of chains and silence. Women, the poor, Indigenous peoples, and the enslaved were denied even the illusion of a vote.

And yet, the march continued. From suffragettes to civil rights activists, from reformers to revolutionaries, the history of democracy is the history of pushing against the boundaries of what was allowed. Every gain—every vote won, every right secured—came not from the kindness of those in power, but from the courage of those who challenged it.

But now, in the 21st century, something has gone wrong. The fire burns low. The passion is fading. Why? Because too many believe that the destination has been reached—that with the rise of political parties, democracy has achieved its final form. The banners are raised, the structures built, the game set. All that's left is to choose sides and cheer. But this is a lie—a dangerous lie.

Party dominance has not expanded democracy. It has strangled it. The menu of options presented to voters grows more bland, more rehearsed, more detached from reality with each passing year.

If democracy is indeed a journey—a path toward collective self-rule, shaped by each generation—then to remain shackled to the party system is to sit down and refuse to walk any further. It is surrender, cloaked in ceremony.

We owe it to the past—and to the future—to keep moving. And that means questioning the monuments we've built. Especially when those monuments block the road forward.

If democracy is not dead, then it must evolve. If the ideal is self-government by the people, then we must stop outsourcing it to factions. A No-Party democracy is the long-overdue correction to a system that has veered off course.

Let's be clear: this is not a call for chaos. It is a call for clarity. For honesty. For alignment between the promise of democracy and its practice. A No-Party system does not discard debate, diversity, or ideology.

No democratic model—whether based on parties or free of them—can escape a simple truth: most human beings are not political theorists. The majority are naturally self-interested, focused on their families, livelihoods, and day-to-day survival. Many are politically naive, shaped more by tabloid headlines, social media influencers, and emotional soundbites than by policy analysis or historical context.

This isn't a flaw in democracy—it's a feature of being human. But what exacerbates this is the deliberate manipulation by the entrenched elite. They have perfected the art of controlling public perception through mass media, crafting narratives that serve their interests. Algorithm-driven distractions keep us glued to screens, consuming shallow content that overwhelms our capacity for deep thought. Censorship, disguised as "safety," stifles genuine debate, while entertainment culture lulls society into passivity. In this environment, the majority become so caught up in being entertained that they forget how to think critically—and how to demand the kind of governance that serves them, not the powerful few.

And yet, this same majority routinely shows sound judgment when it comes to matters that directly affect them. When they face criminal charges, they seek the best lawyer they can afford. When their health is on the line, they look for the most skilled and trustworthy doctor available. Why? Because they understand, instinctively, that competence and alignment matter when the stakes are personal.

That same instinct applies to political representation—when the system allows it. Even those who appear politically disinterested often feel very strongly about at least one issue. A person may never read a policy paper, but still hold firm views on immigration, housing, education, or law enforcement. These convictions may not be shaped by ideology, but they are rooted in real-life experience. And when people recognise that they can elect someone who shares those convictions—someone who is, in some sense, "one of their kind"—the motivation to participate becomes much stronger.

Even the naivest voter understands, at a basic level, that elected representatives vote for or against legislation. They don't need a political science degree to grasp that outcomes are shaped by decisions made on their behalf. And just as they would choose a lawyer who shares their sense of justice or a doctor who respects their values, they want a representative whose beliefs match their own—someone they can trust to speak for them when it matters.

Party systems distort this relationship. They offer voters a brand, not a person. Candidates are selected, controlled, and disciplined by centralised party structures. The voter is asked to trust a logo—not an individual voice. And even if a candidate shares the voter's beliefs, the party whip may prevent that person from ever acting on them.

In a No-Party system, that dynamic changes. The voter chooses an individual—not a party machine. There is no national platform to conform to, no whip to follow. The representative is accountable directly to the people who elected them.

Disinterest and misinformation will always exist, but a No-Party system does not rely on them for survival. Instead, it offers a framework where even minimal political engagement—even a single-issue concern—can lead to a meaningful vote. People may not study policy in depth, but they can still make sound choices about who should speak for them.

Once each constituency sends its own independent representative to parliament—someone chosen for their personal values, judgement, and alignment with the local community—representation becomes almost direct. These individuals are there to reflect the diverse views of the people who elected them. Each seat in the chamber becomes a voice for a real community. In this way, No-Party democracy restores the foundational principle of representation: that elected officials serve the people.

Yes, there will be challenges. No human system is flawless. But compare those challenges to the rot we've normalised under party rule—corruption, inertia, disillusionment, policy dictated by the highest bidder. What we face now is not just imperfect; it is broken. And the longer we pretend otherwise, the more damage is done.

No-Party democracy is not about silencing ideas—it's about unshackling them. It doesn't erase ideology; it demands that ideas stand on their own. It levels the playing field so that no voice is silenced before it speaks, and no dissent is buried.

This is not utopia. It's a repair—a democratic realignment. It is the rediscovery of first principles. That government should reflect the will of the people. That public office is a trust, not a trophy. That democracy, real democracy, must be fought for—not just once in history, but again and again, in every generation.

In summary: political parties are not sacred guardians of democracy; they are historical constructs that have outlived their usefulness and betrayed their purpose. Democracy is not a finished structure but an evolving path—a living project that demands reform when the system ossifies.

The party system, far from guiding that journey, now blocks the road. The first step forward is seeing the cage. The next is walking free.

That path leads to a No-Party system—where the people speak directly, and the representatives they choose serve without faction or filter. The fight for democracy has always been a fight against monopolies of power. Breaking the party cartel is not the end of that struggle. It is its next great chapter.

CHAPTER 12

A Blueprint for Real Democracy

Designing a Responsive System for Any Economy

At the heart of every struggle for justice—whether under capitalism or socialism—lies a simple and universal ideal: that power should reside with the people. This is the promise that gives democracy its moral force. It is also the promise that socialism once claimed it would deliver more fully than capitalism ever could. For much of the twentieth century, millions placed their hopes in socialist movements, believing that public ownership and collective planning would eliminate exploitation and empower the ordinary citizen.

But that promise was never fulfilled. Despite its noble ideals, socialism in practice failed to restore power to the people. The economic system may have changed, but the structure of control did not. Ruling parties simply replaced ruling classes. And while imperial powers undoubtedly worked to destabilise many of these regimes, the failure was not only external. It was structural. A system that concentrates power in the hands of a permanent political elite, and offers no legal way for the public to remove them, is not democratic—no matter what its founding ideology.

In capitalist democracies, a different illusion took hold. The public is told they can change the system with their vote—but what happens when all major parties are already captured? In most modern democracies, the ruling elite has entrenched itself not just in government, but across state institutions: the media, the education system, the intelligence services, and even the judiciary. Elections become exercises in brand-switching between factions of the same elite class. And while faces may change, core policies—on war, finance, surveillance, and inequality—remain untouched.

In so-called socialist regimes like China or Cuba, the situation is more overt: there is no party competition at all. The ruling party is the state. The public cannot vote them out because no legal alternative exists. Elections, where held, are not instruments of change—they are rituals of control, choreographed to reinforce the permanence of the regime. While the slogans differ, the underlying pattern is the same: power is monopolised, and the people are locked out.

In capitalist democracies, there at least remains a peaceful and legal path through which the democratic system can evolve. The Coalition of Independents represents a compelling alternative to party-based governance: a transitional, No-Party democratic movement aimed at restoring public control over public institutions.

The principle is straightforward: elect independent representatives who are accountable solely to the voters in their geographically defined constituencies. The objective is not merely to diversify the political class, but to break down the institutional architecture that compels it to serve interests other than those of the public.

Of course, the system cannot be transformed overnight. Political parties dominate every aspect of the current structure—from ballot access and campaign finance to legislative procedures and media coverage. But their grip is not as unshakeable as it may seem. The cracks are more subtle, but they are there.

Elected representatives, who initially manage to secure nominations within major parties, often find that their role is little more than to rubber-stamp decisions and take orders from party leaders. They quickly realise that their power is limited, and the democratic process is reduced to a mere formality. When they attempt to challenge this, they encounter the full weight of the system, where any dissent is quickly quashed.

This frustration isn't isolated. Across democracies, elected officials have walked away from their positions, citing broken promises and systemic corruption. Some resign; others continue as independents—not out of weakness, but out of principle. They recognise that switching parties won't solve the problem. In systems where real change requires elite sponsorship or massive financial backing, most feel trapped. Parties that challenge entrenched interests are quickly marginalised, defamed, or pacified.

We've seen this play out repeatedly. In Greece, Syriza rose from the ashes of economic collapse, only to surrender to international lenders once in power. In Bolivia, Evo Morales's MAS movement—grounded in indigenous and working-class resistance—won elections but still faced a U.S.-backed coup that removed him despite democratic legitimacy. Even in Spain, Podemos gained momentum in the wake of crisis, only to be gradually neutralised through internal divisions and systemic pressure.

These rare breakthroughs don't signal a healthy system—they expose how broken it is. Without a crisis to crack open the status quo, and without deep insulation from elite influence, movements without establishment backing are rarely allowed to thrive. Even when they win power, they are cornered, compromised, or crushed.

This disillusionment extends beyond legislatures. Influential journalists, civic leaders, former candidates, and ordinary citizens all recognise that something is deeply wrong with the system, but they feel powerless against it. The only "legitimate" paths forward seem to be those sanctioned by the very institutions the public has lost trust in.

But this is an illusion. A trick of the system, like a circle drawn in biro around an ant. The insect thinks it's trapped by a wall, when in truth, the boundary is imaginary. And once it steps outside, it never returns to the false prison again. So too with democracy. As soon as voters and candidates stop accepting the authority of parties, the system begins to unravel.

The roadmap is evolutionary, not revolutionary. It does not begin with overthrowing the system, but with a simple act of defiance:

stop voting for parties. Choose independents. Support candidates who speak for their communities. This is the foundation of No-Party democracy—and it is already within reach.

Electing independents is not a symbolic protest; it is a structural intervention. In systems like the UK, where governments require a parliamentary majority, a critical mass of independents could prevent any single party from forming a government without consensus. In presidential systems like the United States, independents can obstruct partisan control of legislation, forcing policies to rise or fall based on their actual merit.

At first, independents may hold the balance of power. But as their numbers grow, they become more than isolated voices. They become the decisive force. In time, they may choose to form a transparent, policy-driven alliance—not a party in the traditional sense, but a collaborative platform committed to ending the party system itself. In parliamentary democracies, such an alliance could rightfully be invited by a head of state—a president or monarch—to form a government. And from that position of executive power, they could begin the process of constitutional transformation.

This includes:

- **Removing party identifiers from ballots;**
- **Reforming campaign finance and banning taxpayer funding of parties;**
- **Redesigning electoral commissions to be No-Party and independent;**
- **Amending constitutional or parliamentary rules to ensure genuine representation;**
- **And where necessary, putting the question directly to the people through national referenda.**

This transformation is legal, peaceful, and democratic. It works within the framework of existing institutions—but repurposes them in service of the people. Like a rope bridge rebuilt plank by plank, it replaces a decaying structure without collapsing the whole.

At its core, democracy is not just a ritual of elections—it is a mechanism of representation, where people choose individuals to speak and act on their behalf. Yet in today's party-dominated systems, this principle is corrupted before a single vote is cast.

The No-Party model corrects this distortion by starting where democracy truly begins: the local community. In this model, individuals campaign under their own names and ideas, presenting their own priorities to voters. Each candidate publishes a personal manifesto, often structured around ten clear and specific pledges, addressing both local concerns and broader national issues.

This changes the very DNA of politics. Representatives have one duty only: to serve the people who elected them. Re-election is earned through performance, transparency, and integrity. And if they fail? They stand alone—fully answerable to their constituents for every broken promise. In a No-Party system, every election becomes a genuine test of local confidence, national vision, and personal credibility.

This transformation won't come from institutions that profit from the current system—it will come when enough people stop playing by its rules. The spark will come from a convergence of voices: journalists exposing party failures, public figures questioning the system itself, and ordinary voters refusing to legitimise institutions that no longer serve them.

Social media makes this convergence possible on a scale never seen before. When high-trust voices with large followings begin to say, *"Vote Independents—Not Puppets,"* the idea spreads. Communities begin backing independent candidates. Influencers begin promoting pledge-based representation. Voters begin demanding accountability from individuals. That is the turning point. What begins as a movement of resistance becomes a new democratic framework—one built from the ground up.

But electing independents is only the beginning. Once inside the system, they will face an entrenched ruling class determined to protect its grip on power. Dismantling the current party-controlled system will not happen overnight—nor will it follow a clean, predictable path. The journey will be long, uneven, and met with fierce resistance.

History teaches us that ruling elites never surrender power without a fight. Just as capitalist powers once launched full-spectrum campaigns—from regime change abroad to welfare concessions at home—to contain the spread of socialism, so too will today's political establishment fight to preserve the party system. Legal obstructions, media smears, manufactured scandals, and co-opted reform narratives will all be deployed to discredit and divide the movement.

That is why the Coalition of Independents is not just a political idea—it is a strategic formation. A broad alliance of voters, journalists, academics, disillusioned politicians, and public figures—united not by ideology, but by the shared belief that true representation can only begin where parties end.

As this coalition grows in influence, it will evolve—navigating obstacles, countering elite resistance, and adapting its tactics without abandoning its goal. It does not pretend to map every step—only to offer a clear destination.

And with that foundation, we can now move to the next question: If representatives are elected independently—how then do we choose national leaders? In a genuine democracy, the path to executive leadership should be built on merit, public trust, and service.

In the Coalition of Independents model, the process begins with those independently elected representatives. Any representative can nominate a candidate for national leadership, including themselves, provided they secure a minimum threshold of supporting nominations. This isn't a free-for-all—it's structured to ensure candidates have broad-based backing from a chamber of merit-selected individuals. While no system is entirely immune to influence, this model makes elite capture significantly more difficult:

- **First, nominations require support from independently elected MPs or congresspersons—each with their own voter base and no shared loyalty.**

- Second, even after nomination, candidates must face a public general election. They must earn trust directly.
- Third, consensus must be built one policy at a time—a structural check on power from within.
- Fourth, each election cycle in this model brings the possibility of widespread legislative turnover. The composition of parliament is regularly refreshed—creating a kind of automatic reset that makes long-term capture exponentially harder.

This layered accountability doesn't just make capture of the system more challenging; it disrupts it. It replaces predictability with uncertainty. It denies centralized actors the levers they rely on, making manipulation not just harder to execute—but harder to sustain, conceal, or repeat.

How No-Party systems might operate in parliamentary and presidential democracies

In most parliamentary systems today—such as the United Kingdom—the leader of the party that secures a majority of seats in a general election typically becomes the head of government, or Prime Minister. While the public votes for local representatives, the choice of Prime Minister ultimately depends on internal party dynamics, including leadership contests and candidate selection processes.

A No-Party model envisions a fundamentally different approach, one that allows leadership to emerge through open competition, deliberation, and public choice. Once the new Parliament is formed, the process of selecting a Prime Minister might unfold as follows:

1. **Election of Independent Representatives:** Citizens elect a national Parliament composed entirely of independent Members of Parliament (MPs), each standing on their own platform and merit.

2. **Nomination of Prime Ministerial Candidates:** Following the election, MPs nominate candidates from among themselves to stand for Prime Minister. A public, transparent nomination threshold ensures only serious contenders move forward.
3. **Debate and Shortlisting:** The nominated candidates participate in structured parliamentary debates. Successive rounds of voting by MPs narrow the field to two final candidates with the broadest support across the chamber.
4. **National Election:** The final two candidates are presented to the public in a nationwide election. The winner becomes Prime Minister.

The runner-up in the national vote becomes the Shadow Prime Minister-not as a party rival, but as an independent figure empowered to scrutinize the executive and lead opposition in the public interest.

The Shadow Prime Minister is responsible for:

- **Challenging government decisions and holding the Prime Minister to account**
- **Leading public communication on alternative policies**
- **Coordinating with MPs to build opposition to flawed legislation**
- **Forming a Shadow Cabinet of independent MPs and advisors**

This Shadow Cabinet mirrors the official Cabinet and plays a key institutional role in:

- **Analysing and critiquing proposed legislation**
- **Offering alternative proposals and public briefings**
- **Supporting MPs in demanding amendments or voting down government bills**

By providing a structured, credible counterbalance, the Shadow Prime Minister and Shadow Cabinet ensure that all legislation is properly challenged, and executive power remains accountable to Parliament and the public.

The Prime Minister forms a Cabinet by selecting individuals from across the chamber-based on expertise, merit, and alignment with their policy priorities. With no party constraints, this pool of independent MPs allows for broader and more representative governance.

Unlike in party systems, there is no formal "opposition party." Instead, each policy proposal must win support from a majority of independently elected MPs-based on open debate, evidence, and public interest, not party loyalty or enforced discipline.

Where upper chambers exist-such as the House of Lords in the UK-these would also be reformed to operate on a No-Party basis. Appointments would continue based on expertise and public contribution, but Lords would act independently, free from party influence.

This No-Party parliamentary model offers a range of democratic and structural improvements:

- **No party gatekeeping:** Leadership emerges from open competition.
- **Direct public mandate:** Both the Prime Minister and Shadow Prime Minister receive democratic legitimacy through national public votes.
- **Transparent opposition:** A formal Shadow Cabinet provides structured scrutiny without partisan obstructionism.
- **Stronger representation:** MPs vote independently, guided by evidence, policy, and constituent interests.
- **Better governance:** Cabinet appointments are based on competence and collaboration.
- **Reduced polarization:** The absence of party divisions encourages issue-based debate and consensus-building.

How No-Party Systems Might Operate in Presidential Democracies

In most presidential systems-such as the United States-the President is elected directly by the public. However, the path to the presidency is typically shaped by political parties. A No-Party model reimagines presidential elections without political parties.

Just like in the parliamentary version of this model, the process begins with a general election in which voters elect local representatives. Every candidate for the legislature runs as an independent. Once a No-Party legislature is formed, the process of selecting a President proceeds as follows:

1. **Election of Independent Representatives: Citizens elect a national legislative chamber made up entirely of independent local representatives through a general election. The U.S. Senate continues to operate in its current form. However, all Senate elections are No-Party, and Senators serve independently.**
2. Presidential Nomination: Any eligible citizen may seek nomination for the presidency but must first secure the backing of a minimum number of elected representatives.
3. Debate and Shortlisting: The nominated candidates participate in public debates and policy discussions. Elected representatives engage in rounds of deliberative voting to narrow the field to two final candidates with the broadest support in the chamber.
4. Running Mate Selection: Prior to the national election, each of the two presidential finalists selects a Vice Presidential running mate. The public then votes for the Presidential-Vice Presidential ticket.
5. National Election: The top two candidates are presented to the public in a nationwide general election. The

> winning ticket forms the executive branch, with the President holding a direct and personal mandate from the electorate.

The runner-up in the national vote assumes the formal role of Shadow President-not as a partisan rival, but as an independent figure with a constitutional mandate to scrutinize the executive and uphold democratic accountability.

The Shadow President is responsible for:

- Monitoring executive actions and government performance
- Leading public inquiries or investigations
- Communicating directly with the public on matters of national importance
- Forming a Shadow Cabinet

This Shadow Cabinet mirrors the official Cabinet and plays a critical institutional role in:

- Analysing and critiquing proposed legislation and executive policies
- Providing alternative policy proposals and public briefings
- Supporting independent legislators in demanding amendments or voting down flawed bills

By organizing structured, informed opposition to government proposals, the Shadow President and Shadow Cabinet ensure that all legislation is thoroughly examined-not just by the executive, but by a parallel team with a public mandate to hold power to account.

Once elected, the President forms an official Cabinet by appointing individuals based on merit, expertise, and alignment with their policy agenda. As in the current U.S. system, these appointments are subject to approval by both chambers of Congress, including the Senate, which continues to perform its constitutional oversight and confirmation duties.

All legislative business—including Cabinet confirmations, policy debates, and voting on bills—is carried out by independent legislators. With no party blocs or whips, support for any proposal must be built through public reasoning, negotiation, and persuasion on the merits of each issue.

This No-Party presidential model offers several democratic and structural advantages:

- No party gatekeeping: Leadership is open to any qualified individual with the backing of elected representatives.
- Balanced accountability: A formal Shadow President and Shadow Cabinet create transparent, structured oversight of the executive.
- Stronger representation: Legislators act independently on behalf of constituents.
- Better governance: Executive appointments and decisions are made on merit and public interest.
- Less polarization: Without party identity dominating every issue, the political focus shifts toward solving real problems through evidence and reason.
- A clear public mandate: Both the President and Shadow President receive democratic legitimacy through direct public election.
- Constitutional continuity: The role of the Senate, the structure of executive power, and public elections remain intact.

This model does not aim to rewrite foundational constitutional arrangements-particularly federal balances, but rather to restore responsiveness and integrity where party dominance has weakened both.

Unlike today's opposition parties—driven by political rivalry and campaign strategy—the Shadow Executive offers transparent, evidence-based oversight. Their role is not to obstruct, but to contribute:

- Highlighting legal, ethical, or practical flaws in proposed legislation
- Presenting the public with clear, unfiltered perspectives
- Equipping independent representatives with rigorous counterarguments before key votes

This reform doesn't just change who wins. It changes how leadership operates—and how power is held to account.

In the party-based system:

- Accountability is often delayed—only arriving after scandal or public outrage.
- Media narratives dominate over rational, fact-based discussion.
- Opposition parties critique policies not to improve them, but to win the next election.

In the No-Party model:

- Oversight is continuous and institutionalised
- Debate is grounded in evidence, not tribal loyalty
- Both the executive and Shadow Executive are democratically chosen, judged on merit, and accountable in real time

A No-Party democracy offers what party systems so often fail to provide: strong government *and* strong opposition—simultaneously. Executive leadership is formed through consensus among independently elected representatives. This enables stable governance rooted in merit and public trust, while preserving a diverse, issue-based opposition capable of scrutiny without sabotage.

By contrast, party-based democracies swing between two extremes—paralysis or domination—depending on the electoral system.

In proportional representation systems, the result is often legislative fragmentation. No single party wins a majority, forcing coalition governments made up of ideologically divergent factions. These coalitions are frequently unstable and paralysed by compromise, with parties abandoning core manifesto pledges just to stay in power. Worse still, small or extremist factions can gain outsized influence by threatening to collapse the coalition unless their demands are met.

Israel provides a clear example. Coalition governments there often rely on ultra-Orthodox or far-right minority parties, who wield disproportionate power over national policy despite limited electoral support. The result is gridlock, brinkmanship, and repeated snap elections—governance held hostage by factional bargaining.

In first-past-the-post systems like the United Kingdom, the danger flips. When a single party secures a strong parliamentary majority, it gains near-total control of the legislative process. The opposition, no matter how principled or popular, is rendered effectively powerless. Policies can be passed without genuine scrutiny.

In both systems, power becomes either fractured or absolute—leaving the public with instability or unaccountable rule.

No-Party democracy offers a more balanced alternative: stability without suppression, and clarity without conformity. When the government introduces legislation, it must present it to the full chamber. There is no guaranteed majority.

The Shadow Cabinet plays a vital role: scrutinising proposals, exposing weaknesses, and offering constructive amendments. Reasonable improvements may be adopted. Flawed laws may be rejected. This creates a genuine balance of power: The executive governs. The shadow scrutinises. The chamber decides. Opposition is structural—a permanent safeguard, not a placeholder for the next election.

Defenders of the party system often argue that without political parties, legislatures would descend into disorder. They claim that parties are essential for providing structure, coordination, and the continuity needed for effective governance. Without them, they warn, policymaking would fragment, alliances would shift unpredictably, and governments would become paralysed.

Yet this concern reflects entrenched assumptions rather than evidence. Party-based systems may appear orderly, but much of that "order" is the product of enforced conformity, not genuine consensus. What is typically celebrated as legislative stability often rests on rigid discipline—serving party interests rather than the public will.

In the United Kingdom, Members of Parliament routinely vote on legislation they have not read, do not fully understand, or may fundamentally oppose—compelled by the party whip to follow leadership directives. Former Conservative MP and cabinet minister Rory Stewart—who served in several senior roles, including Secretary of State for International Development—has described Parliament as a "zombie chamber," where MPs shuffle through voting lobbies like automatons, constrained by hierarchy rather than guided by informed judgment.

The United States offers a parallel picture. Bills are frequently crafted behind closed doors by party-aligned committees, often in collaboration with lobbyists, and then pushed through Congress on party-line votes. Representatives are expected to fall in line with leadership, regardless of their constituents' views or their own policy understanding.

A No-Party model would replace this with a system centred on deliberation and accountability. Leadership would still exist—through a Prime Minister or President and a formal Shadow counterpart—both selected by the elected legislature.

These leaders would continue to perform the core functions associated with executive government and opposition—proposing legislation, articulating national priorities, and providing scrutiny.

Elected representatives would be free to assess each proposal on its merits. Crucially, they would not be punished or expelled for voting according to conscience. In contrast to current systems, No-Party representatives would vote yes or no based on substance, not strategy.

This is not a prescription for chaos. On the contrary, it is a path toward more grounded and effective governance. Legislative outcomes may be less predictable, but they are also more likely to reflect reasoned debate and public interest. The No-Party model transforms today's stagnant, tribal system into one of real, dynamic governance—where **debate, independence, and public accountability** are at the core.

Here's how it works:

- **Representatives vote based on their own judgment and the pledges they made to their constituents.**
- **Informal alliances may form around specific issues—like healthcare, housing, or education—but these are voluntary and policy-driven.**
- **Every bill must earn support through persuasion, public justification, and open scrutiny.**

Will this slow things down? **maybe.** But that's not dysfunction—that's **deliberation.**

Where party systems push legislation through to meet political calendars or media cycles, the No-Party model gives representatives the time—and responsibility—to **read, understand, and justify** what they vote for.

And that doesn't mean each representative must become an expert on every issue. That's where the **Shadow Executive** plays a crucial role. For every major proposal, the Shadow President or Shadow Prime Minister presents a **formal counterposition**—offering analysis, critique, and alternative solutions.

Representatives no longer need to rely on spin or party briefings. They can **hear both sides**, weigh the arguments, and vote accordingly. This leads to:

- Fewer bloated omnibus bills passed under pressure.
- More focused, transparent legislation shaped by genuine consensus.
- A system where constituents finally know why their representative voted a certain way.

In a No-Party chamber, **every vote is an act of judgment**. And every law must stand on its **merits**.

In party-based systems, top government roles are often handed out as rewards—for loyalty, campaign support, or ideological obedience.

In the UK, the Prime Minister must choose Cabinet ministers from their party's pool of elected MPs. This already limits the talent available—and within that narrow pool, appointments often go to factional allies rather than the most capable hands.

In the US, the President is not bound to choose from among elected officials. In theory, this allows for a broader and more merit-based selection. But in practice, the Cabinet often fills with donors, lobbyists, campaign insiders, or ideological enforcers—so long as they can pass Senate confirmation. The result is the same: cronyism cloaked as leadership.

In a No-Party UK Parliament, the Prime Minister is no longer limited to a party's MPs. Every independently elected representative is a potential Cabinet member. In a No-Party US Congress, Senators evaluate Cabinet nominees on merit.

Experts from across public service, academia, and civil society can be brought in. And because the process is transparent, the public can see each appointment unfold.

This is what competent democracy should look like: governance without faction—and leadership without compromise. Across democracies—whether in the United States, the UK, Canada, Germany, or India—the core reform principle remains constant: Shift representation from party machines to independent individuals accountable directly to the public.

The No-Party model does not seek to clone a single structure across all nations. It recognises that democracy is a living organism, shaped by history and culture. But across systems, one truth holds: At the root of every modern democratic failure lies one common cause—the party system. It is the party machine—not the constitution—that:

- Blocks accountability
- Suppresses local voice
- Centralises power
- Enables elite capture

By removing the party filter, we restore what was supposed to be foundational:

- Citizens regaining ownership of their representatives
- Institutions regaining their integrity and function
- Governance serving public trust

Every system of governance would have some flaws. But the party-based model is not just flawed, It is engineered for control. No system is immune to corruption. But not every system is equally vulnerable. In a party-based model, corruption is centralised.

In a No-Party model, corruption becomes exponentially harder:

- There's no party infrastructure to hijack.
- Donors must corrupt one representative at a time—publicly, and under local scrutiny.
- No one can hide behind "we were just following orders."
- Every representative is exposed—their votes, their promises, their donors—all in plain sight.

This doesn't mean wrongdoing disappears. But it becomes harder to organise, easier to detect, and impossible to industrialise.

When voters no longer have to guess which faction their representative serves … When laws are debated openly and justified clearly ... When every election is a contest of character ... Then democracy is no longer a ritual. It becomes what it was meant to be: A system rooted in honesty, accountability, and shared power.

Chapter 13

Break the Chains, Not the System

*Disempowering Parties
by Refusing to Vote for Them*

DEMOCRACY DOESN'T NEED to be destroyed—it needs to be reclaimed. The problem isn't the structure of elections or representative government; it's the machinery of party politics that distorts it. For too long, voters have been told their only choice is which party to support, not whether parties should control the system at all. But power only exists where we consent to give it. By refusing to vote for any political party, citizens can peacefully but decisively withdraw that consent—not to break democracy, but to liberate it from the chains of factional control. A No-Party system begins not with revolution, but with a refusal.

Rejecting parties is a necessary step toward decentralising power—but it is not a guarantee of virtue. A No-Party system can reduce systemic corruption, yet it cannot erase the more basic truths of human behaviour.

No democratic model—whether structured around political parties or built without them—can afford to ignore the realities of human nature. Power attracts ambition. Influence invites manipulation. Wealth seeks access. And individuals, however well-intentioned, remain susceptible to pressure, persuasion, and self-interest. These traits do not disappear in a No-Party system. Removing parties does not eliminate ambition or corruption. This book does not claim otherwise.

The difference lies not in the nature of people, but in the design of the system. Party-based democracies concentrate power, centralise decision-making, and offer predictable pathways for control. No-Party systems, by contrast, disperse authority, remove enforcement mechanisms like party discipline, and complicate elite manipulation. While the motivations of actors remain unchanged, the tools available to them—and the terrain they must navigate—are fundamentally different.

This structural difference matters. Critics are right to be cautious about grand reformist claims. They've seen revolutions promise justice, only to create new elites. They've watched campaign finance reforms pass, while corporate money rerouted itself through super PACs. They've seen parties once committed to workers or civil rights become polished platforms of elite consensus. So when a new system is proposed—one that removes parties entirely—the natural question arises: "What stops it from becoming the same thing under a different name?"

It's a fair question. And the answer is not that corruption disappears. It's that the current structures making corruption efficient, scalable, and protected—especially centralised party control—are dismantled. The No-Party model doesn't eliminate corruption. It disrupts the machinery that sustains it. Corruption becomes less coordinated, less predictable, and much harder to institutionalise.

Dispersing Power—Why Design Matters

In party systems, corruption has infrastructure. There is a ladder of leadership to climb, a donor network to enter, a national strategy to follow, and a whip system to ensure loyalty. A small group at the top can make decisions that shape the lives of millions. No-Party systems remove these conduits. Influence may still exist, but it must pass through hundreds of independently elected representatives—each without party gatekeeping or enforced ideological loyalty.

This decentralisation changes the political calculus. Elite actors may still try to buy influence, but their returns become uncertain. Coordination fragments. Representatives are accountable not to a party centre or manifesto, but to their local constituents. The space for quiet capture shrinks.

But what about over time? The greater threat isn't immediate corruption, but gradual erosion. What stops independently elected officials from informally aligning, forming blocs, and eventually reconstituting into factions or even full-fledged parties? If power abhors a vacuum, won't new structures naturally form to fill it?

The answer lies in designing a system that discourages permanence and rewards fluidity. The problem with party systems is not that people agree. Agreement is healthy and expected. The problem arises when these agreements solidify into permanent, state-supported institutions—complete with public funding, legal protections, ideological enforcement, and exclusive electoral privileges. That is the danger.

The No-Party system does not outlaw collaboration. It anticipates it. Representatives will align on issues, build coalitions, and propose common strategies—just as in any healthy democracy. But these alliances remain temporary and issue-based. They do not access state funding, share a legal identity, or enforce loyalty through whips or internal sanctions. The system breaks the moment cooperation becomes coercion.

Safeguards are embedded: no party names on ballots, no legal registration for parties, no whip powers, and no guaranteed parliamentary advantages based on group size. In this way, the system acknowledges factionalism as a natural political tendency—but refuses to grant it legal status or structural advantage. Just as free markets require anti-monopoly laws, democratic systems require protections against permanent political monopolies.

No-Party democracy is not about eliminating collective action. It is about ensuring that collective action remains just that—collective action, not institutionalised into legal structures that dominate the political landscape. After all, this is precisely what the Founding Fathers feared: that temporary alliances would harden into permanent factions, distorting the will of the people and corrupting the republic.

Crucially, this model does not pretend perfection. It does not claim to create flawless representatives or frictionless politics. Instead, it shifts the centre of gravity away from hierarchical control and toward openness. Elite capture becomes harder. Independent voices gain space. Political legitimacy comes not from branding, but from direct connection to voters.

Corruption in politics rarely erupts suddenly. It creeps in strategically. It begins not with bribery, but with an understanding of how power flows, where control resides, and how those points can be gradually captured. Party-based democracies make this process easier. They centralise power, enforce internal discipline, and offer a direct pipeline for elite influence—from donors to party leaders, from party leaders to legislators, and from legislators to law. Over time, this creates a self-sustaining loop of influence.

Consider the United Kingdom. The Labour Party began with roots in trade unions and working-class representation. But after union power was weakened by legislation during the Thatcher era, corporate interests filled the vacuum. By the 1990s, under New Labour, the party actively courted financial elites. Donors began shaping the agenda. The working-class voice was diluted in favour of elite consensus.

A parallel unfolded in the United States. Both the Democratic and Republican parties once had strong local bases and ideological diversity. But from the 1970s onward, corporate influence surged. Beginning with the Powell Memo and solidified through rulings like Buckley v. Valeo and Citizens United, money became the defining force in politics. Today, both parties operate within elite donor ecosystems, their agendas shaped less by public need and more by financial patronage.

This isn't coincidental. It reveals a design flaw in the party system. Once elites gain control of a party, the system helps them stay there. Internal hierarchies and enforcement tools protect the status quo. Dissent is filtered out. Party loyalty becomes a prerequisite for political survival. Change, when it comes, is symbolic.

No-Party democracy is built to resist this. It isn't utopian. It does not presume the virtue of all representatives. Instead, it relies on structural friction. By removing party hierarchies, it dismantles the machinery that enables sustained elite capture.

Earned Leadership—Ending the Pipeline of Pre-Selection

Take leadership selection. In a party system, leaders are not chosen by the public but elevated from within. Candidates are groomed, filtered, and approved by strategists and donors long before any public vote. By the time voters see them, the options are already pre-selected.

In a No-Party system, this top-down process is eliminated. National leadership begins with independently elected representatives. Any representative can nominate themselves or others, provided they gather enough nominations from fellow independents. It is these representatives who determine the final list of leadership candidates. Even the most well-funded candidate cannot guarantee nomination. There is no party apparatus to enforce outcomes.

And what happens if an elite-backed candidate does make it into office? In party systems, a president or prime minister brings with them a loyal legislative bloc. They rely on party discipline to drive policy. Whips secure obedience. Dissenters are punished. Votes are treated as obligations, not deliberations.

In a No-Party system, even a sitting leader has no guaranteed legislative power. They cannot command votes. There is no party majority. Every bill must be debated and justified. Representatives vote on merit, not loyalty. Authority must be earned, not assumed.

This difference is profound in both parliamentary and presidential systems. In a parliamentary democracy like the UK, the executive typically controls the legislature through the party. If a party holds a majority, its leader governs with sweeping power. In contrast, presidential systems like the U.S. separate executive and legislative authority. Yet even here, presidents often use executive orders or administrative tools to bypass opposition.

No-Party democracy changes this dynamic. A president still has power, but no guaranteed defenders. Every initiative must be justified. Every action is scrutinised. Legislators are free to investigate, oppose, or support based on judgment, not allegiance.

This is the essence of structural resilience. Decentralisation isn't just an ideal. It's a defence mechanism. Without whips, every vote must be earned. Without party labels, candidates stand on their own record. Without central leadership, there is no throne to seize.

Perhaps the most vital point is this: in party systems, capture is sticky. Once elites gain control of a party, they rarely lose it. They dominate nominations, shape media access, and filter out dissenting voices. Even public dissatisfaction struggles to break through. The system preserves itself.

No-Party systems resist that entrenchment. There is no party to capture. No central platform to defend. Every seat is contested anew. Every representative stands as an individual. Influence cannot be passed on or inherited. It must be rebuilt each time.

Corruption may still arise. But party systems lock it in. No-Party systems interrupt it by design. And in an era defined by elite influence and widespread disillusionment, that interruption is not just preferable—it may be democracy's best remaining safeguard.

The most persistent and legitimate concern about No-Party systems is not whether they can function—but whether they can remain No-Party. Humans are social and political beings. We seek allies. We form groups. We rally around shared goals. Even in the absence of formal parties, what prevents informal blocs from evolving into structured parties over time?

The answer is not to ban political collaboration—but to design systems that prevent it from ossifying into exclusive control. Factions are natural. What matters is whether they can transform into institutionalised gatekeepers. The danger is not shared beliefs. The danger is when those beliefs are given legal privileges—the right to dominate ballots, access state funds, enforce internal discipline, or exclude dissent. That's the road from a faction to a party. And that's the road the No-Party model blocks by design.

Factions will form. Some will be fleeting, others long-lasting. They might coalesce around economic ideology, religious values, environmental concerns, or national identity. But permanence alone is not the problem. The problem is when that permanence hardens into a structural monopoly over representation.

Party-based systems enable that hardening. No-Party systems do not. The critical difference lies in legal and procedural recognition. Political parties in most democracies are state-recognised entities. They receive public funding, enjoy branded ballot access, shape media coverage, and enforce loyalty through whips and internal rules.

No-Party systems deliberately deny factions this legal pathway. They may campaign, coordinate, and endorse—but they cannot:

- **Appear on ballots under a shared name or logo**
- **Access public funding as a bloc**
- **Whip votes or enforce discipline**
- **Field candidates under a unified platform**
- **Gain procedural privileges in legislatures or media**

Their influence remains persuasive, not institutional. Structural, not legal. They are coalitions of advocacy, not engines of control.

This has profound consequences. Without party labels, the ballot paper levels the field. Voters engage with candidates as individuals. Even candidates who share a worldview compete for trust, not ride a shared platform. Factional alignment becomes an open conversation, not a closed pipeline.

Inside legislatures, coordination remains possible—but not enforceable. Factions cannot claim floor time, dictate voting blocks, or use their size to lock down procedures. Coalitions are built around issues, and dissolve just as easily. The friction against institutionalisation is deliberate.

Some critics argue that this just drives partisanship underground. That factions will still behave like parties in all but name. But that critique overlooks a vital point: in party systems, partisanship is rewarded with formal power. In No-Party systems, factional influence remains fluid, competitive, and always subject to public judgment. No group can claim ownership of the process.

And because factional identities have no legal anchor, no one can prevent internal disagreement. A broad environmentalist faction may include both radical reformers and pragmatic incrementalists—all standing independently. There is no leadership to enforce conformity or bar dissent.

This is what protects No-Party democracy from reversion. Not a ban on political identity—but the withdrawal of privileges that transform identity into control. The system expects coordination, but prevents it from calcifying. It encourages collaboration, but denies it the power to command.

In this way, No-Party democracy guards against its own unravelling. It does not pretend factions will disappear. It ensures they cannot dominate. And that design decision—more than ideology or enforcement—is what sustains the model's resilience.

One of the most pointed criticisms of any democratic reform—especially No-Party democracy—is this: what does any of it matter if concentrated wealth continues to dominate politics? In an age where billionaires can shape public discourse, influence elections, and quietly steer legislation, can political redesign really defend democracy against the force of money?

No political system can entirely eliminate the influence of wealth or power. In any unequal society, those with more resources will always have more reach. But not all systems offer the same level of vulnerability. The critical difference lies in how accessible and entrenched the channels of influence are.

In party-based democracies, capture is efficient. There is a direct pipeline from donor to decision: fund the leadership, secure control of the party agenda, and use internal discipline to pass preferred policies. Once access is gained at the top, influence flows downward with ease.

In contrast, the No-Party model dismantles that shortcut. There is no party leadership to capture, no whip system to coerce votes, no branded bloc to buy. Influence must be exerted across a diverse landscape of independently elected representatives. The cost of capture rises. The certainty of return diminishes.

Importantly, the problem is not capitalism itself. This book does not advocate the end of private enterprise, markets, or wealth creation. Capitalism, for all its flaws, remains the dominant economic framework across much of the world. The issue is the failure of democracy to insulate itself from capitalism's worst distortions. And here, the party system is its softest point.

But this vulnerability is not exclusive to capitalist regimes. In state-led or nominally socialist systems, capture takes a different form: the ruling party becomes the elite. Power is consolidated not by private wealth but by political machinery. The judiciary, the media, even civil society are subordinated to a single institutional force. The result is the same—centralised control, protected from public challenge.

The No-Party system breaks that pattern in both contexts. It prevents the formation of political monopolies—whether by capital or the state. Candidates do not owe their careers to donor networks or ideological enforcement. They emerge from communities, grounded in trust and local accountability. There is no elite filter to pass through.

None of this means money vanishes from politics. Corporate lobbies, billionaire donors, and powerful interest groups will still attempt to shape opinion, support campaigns, and push their agendas. But without the structural tools provided by parties, their influence can no longer be hardwired into government. It must be rebuilt from scratch each election cycle, constituency by constituency. Power becomes harder to concentrate—and easier to challenge.

More importantly, elected representatives in a No-Party system are not bound by party discipline. This frees them to pursue financial reform, challenge monopolies, or advocate for climate justice without fear of internal political retaliation. While individual corruption may still exist, the system itself removes the structural incentives to obey donors, strategists, or party elites.

Even within today's flawed systems, we see flashes of this dynamic. When public pressure becomes politically dangerous to ignore—when it risks fracturing voter blocs or fuelling outsider movements—the establishment scrambles to respond. Nigel Farage's rise through UKIP and the Brexit Party demonstrates this clearly. Though never elected to Westminster, Farage channelled the anger of a disillusioned public. His momentum bled support from the main parties, eventually forcing the ruling government to offer a referendum—not out of principle, but to contain the threat.

Now contrast that with the millions who marched against the Iraq War. Their voices were morally powerful but politically irrelevant. They posed no threat to the system because both major parties backed the war. There was no electoral price for ignoring them—so they were ignored.

In a No-Party democracy, whether it's a local representative or a presidential candidate seeking a national mandate, public will is the only path to power. There are no party shields to hide behind, no donor networks to override grassroots sentiment. Trust must be earned directly. Accountability is not occasional—it is constant.

The No-Party model does not claim to eliminate power disparities. But it reshapes the terrain on which power operates. Whether in capitalist systems, where private wealth gains control, or in socialist or state-led systems, where dominant leaders or factions within ruling parties consolidate authority, the danger lies in permanent political machinery. It is not ruling elites alone, but the party apparatus that enables their grip on power to endure. The No-Party model dismantles this machinery. Without party infrastructure to hijack, representation resets with every election cycle. In place of predictability for those in power, it reintroduces uncertainty—a defining feature of genuine democratic accountability. Influence must be rebuilt from the ground up, forcing power to remain responsive—and vulnerable—to the public will.

A No-Party democracy is not a utopia. It will not eradicate corruption entirely, abolish inequality, or transform every elected official into a paragon of virtue. Human nature—with its ambitions, loyalties, biases, and self-interest—will remain a constant. No system can erase that.

But what a No-Party system can do is rewire the conditions in which human nature plays out. It can disrupt the infrastructure that makes elite capture easy and corruption scalable. It can dismantle the party machinery that rewards obedience over integrity and conformity over competence. And it can replace those dynamics with decentralisation, independence, and public accountability.

This is not about perfecting democracy—it is about maturing it. Party-based democracy is not the end point of democratic evolution. It is a phase that has become calcified. What began as a coordination mechanism has morphed into a gatekeeping apparatus. No-Party democracy represents the next step—a reassertion of what representation was always meant to be: a direct line between citizen and delegate.

This system doesn't promise harmony. It promises openness. It doesn't eliminate conflict. It ensures that conflict remains dynamic and publicly accountable. And most importantly, it re-establishes the connection between elected officials and the people they serve.

It's often said that democracy is the worst form of government—except for all the others. But that line conceals a deeper truth: democracy itself has many forms. Party-based systems are not synonymous with democracy. They are merely one design, and they are overdue for renovation.

No-Party democracy does not mean the absence of disagreement. It means the absence of gatekeepers. It opens the doors to more voices, more debate, and more innovation—not less. And in an era when politics has grown increasingly centralised, performative, and unresponsive, that shift is not just a reform. It is a democratic necessity.

While it is neither possible nor necessary to prescribe every procedural outcome of a No-Party democracy in advance, certain pathways toward institutional renewal can already be envisioned.

A structurally independent legislature and executive—freed from the constraints of party discipline and elite patronage—would possess both the mandate and the capacity to begin reversing the deep-rooted capture of democratic institutions. Through legislation aimed at dismantling media monopolies, securing a diverse and pluralistic private media landscape, and establishing genuinely independent public broadcasters, such a system could reassert democratic control over the information environment. Oversight mechanisms to ensure algorithmic transparency and neutrality on digital platforms would further safeguard the public sphere from manipulation.

Complementary reforms could focus on restoring judicial independence by depoliticising appointments, reorienting national curricula toward critical thinking and civic responsibility, and insulating academic institutions from financial or ideological capture. The objective is not to recreate every institution from the ground up, but rather to analyse how elite actors engineered systemic dominance—through concentrated ownership, narrative control, and institutional gatekeeping—and to legislate accordingly to dismantle these mechanisms.

Within this broader framework, the progressive taxation of political donations emerges as one particularly illustrative reform. It offers a means of counterbalancing disproportionate financial influence without suppressing political participation. More importantly, it demonstrates how a No-Party democracy can implement structural recalibrations that render political power visible, accountable, and grounded in the public interest.

Turning the Tide—Progressively Taxing Donations and Philanthropy

Modern political systems frequently disguise elite control as civic virtue. Political donations are framed as participation, and philanthropy is lauded as generosity. Yet in practice, both have evolved into sophisticated tools for consolidating power, often at the expense of democratic equality.

Though democratic theory is grounded in the principle of political equality—one person, one vote—political reality is frequently shaped by unequal access to influence. Those with the financial means to fund campaigns, lobby representatives, and shape discourse enjoy a level of political power far beyond that available to ordinary citizens. Political donations and charitable foundations have become two central mechanisms by which this imbalance is maintained. In many cases, they operate legally, are tax-advantaged, and remain largely invisible to the public.

By removing the party infrastructure that traditionally served as the primary conduit for elite influence, a No-Party democratic model opens space for institutional reform. However, the absence of parties does not, in itself, eliminate the incentives for capital to shape political outcomes. What it enables is a shift in how political influence is handled—moving from unregulated dominance to a model based on structural disincentives, transparency, and democratic accountability. One of the most promising innovations in this context is the application of progressive taxation to political contributions.

Large-scale political donations are often justified as a form of democratic expression. Advocates argue that supporting candidates or causes is a legitimate form of participation, akin to speech or protest. But when the magnitude of a donation allows one individual or organisation to effectively purchase visibility, control media narratives, or shape the legislative agenda, it ceases to be participation and becomes political leverage. What is being exercised is not opinion, but market power.

Compounding the problem, many systems classify political donations as tax-deductible or treat them as ordinary business expenses. This means that the public is, paradoxically, subsidising the very mechanisms that enable elite domination. Democracy, in such a framework, becomes a subsidised auction—where power accrues to the wealthiest participants.

A No-Party system does not prohibit donations outright. Rather, it redefines their status and consequence. Political donations are no longer treated as inherently virtuous but as attempts to influence public decision-making—attempts that must be subject to proportional obligation.

Under such a framework, small-scale donations—such as those under £500 per individual per election cycle—would be viewed as ordinary civic engagement and would remain untaxed. These are unlikely to distort democratic representation and may even strengthen local participation.

However, as donations increase in size, so too would the donor's financial responsibility. Contributions above certain thresholds—such as £10,000, £50,000, or more—could be taxed at progressively higher rates, potentially reaching or exceeding 50% in cases of large-scale influence. This would not criminalise political donations, but it would impose a meaningful cost on attempts to dominate the political landscape through financial means.

The revenue generated from this influence tax would be allocated to a Democracy Fund. This fund could be used to provide public financing for candidates-without requiring taxpayers to foot the entire bill. Importantly, once the presidential or prime ministerial race is narrowed down to the final two candidates, both would receive equal public funding. This approach is more effective than traditional party-based systems, where, in some proportional representation countries, over ten parties might receive public funding regardless of their actual viability. In this way, elite spending would serve not only to advance a particular candidate or cause but also to strengthen the overall democratic framework by levelling the playing field and reinforcing the integrity of the electoral process.

Transparency is an essential counterpart to taxation. In a No-Party system, all political donations—whether direct to candidates or through third-party organisations—would be subject to real-time disclosure. This includes in-kind support, event sponsorship, and media expenditures. Where contributions exceed a defined threshold, donor names and amounts would be listed on official candidate profiles. In particularly significant cases, such information could also appear directly on the ballot.

The purpose is not to punish donors, but to inform voters. Citizens have the right to know not only who they are voting for, but also which private interests are most invested in that candidate's success.

Beyond direct donations, elite philanthropy has emerged as a dominant and under-regulated avenue of political influence. Through foundations, endowments, and charitable trusts, wealthy individuals can shape public discourse, fund academic research, and influence media narratives—all while remaining outside the regulatory boundaries that apply to explicit political activity.

The Koch network, extensively examined in Jane Mayer's *Dark Money*, illustrates this dynamic with particular clarity. Rather than concentrating solely on campaign finance, the Kochs funded think tanks, endowed academic programs, and supported ideologically aligned media organisations. Their long-term strategy was to build an intellectual and cultural infrastructure capable of influencing policy across multiple generations.

To prevent strategic philanthropy from undermining democratic accountability, a No-Party system would establish clear boundaries between charity and political intervention. Tax exemptions for charitable organisations would be made conditional on non-involvement in political or legislative advocacy. Foundations that engage in such activities—either directly or indirectly—would lose their privileged tax status and be reclassified accordingly.

In addition, large-scale charitable donations—particularly those directed toward universities, think tanks, and media organisations—would be subject to full transparency. Donors and recipients would be required to disclose funding sources, institutional affiliations, and intended policy outcomes. Any organisation that seeks to influence legislation, regulation, or electoral outcomes—regardless of charitable status—would be registered under a public influence framework. These entities would be required to disclose their activities, donor lists, and expenditures through a publicly accessible database.

In a No-Party democracy, the choice to influence public outcomes through wealth would remain available, but it would come with obligations: full disclosure, proportional financial contribution, and visibility rather than concealment.

Just as wealth is taxed to sustain public infrastructure, political influence would be taxed to sustain the democratic commons. A No-Party system does not seek to silence speech or prohibit private giving. It simply rejects the notion that all money is neutral. Through progressive taxation, universal transparency, and ethical regulation, it ensures that influence is no longer hidden, unaccountable, or insulated from public scrutiny.

This redistribution of influence has ripple effects far beyond campaign finance. Other institutions—from environmental agencies to financial regulators—are likewise freed from political subservience. Without the need to conform to party platforms or shield political allies, independent representatives are free to support bold, evidence-based reforms: fairer tax systems, real antitrust enforcement, transparent procurement practices, and climate policy shaped by science, not slogans.

Perhaps most importantly, public policy becomes a matter of deliberation rather than branding. Proposals rise or fall on merit. Laws are passed because they survive scrutiny. Representatives can debate, compromise, and learn—without the looming threat of deselection or internal discipline.

But the most profound reform is cultural. When politics becomes less tribal, public discourse becomes more honest. Without the distorting filter of party identity, citizens are no longer forced to defend every failure of their "side" or reject every idea from the "other." The conversation shifts—from loyalty to outcomes, from rivalry to responsibility. And trust, long corroded by factionalism, begins to rebuild.

No-Party democracy will not resolve every policy disagreement. But it can make those disagreements more transparent, less toxic, and more aligned with the public interest. It creates space—political, institutional, and cultural—where reform is not only possible, but sustainable.

Some sceptics may argue that a No-Party democratic model would be a fragile anomaly—a brief detour before politics inevitably reverts to party-driven rule. While no fully developed No-Party system exists today, the model is designed not simply to function, but to endure.

Its strength lies not in idealism, but in its built-in resistance to consolidation. Unlike party-based systems that centralise authority and entrench power over time, a No-Party framework is engineered for continual renewal. Each election resets the political landscape. Candidates must earn public trust afresh. There is no institutional apparatus to guarantee succession or preserve influence beyond a single term.

This deliberate impermanence is not a weakness; it is the system's greatest defence. By avoiding entrenched hierarchies, factional capture, and ideological monopolies, No-Party democracy reduces the risk of hijacking by special interests or entrenched elites. It creates a political culture where legitimacy must be continuously earned, and where accountability is restored to its rightful place—in the hands of the electorate.

The architecture of No-Party democracy also encourages generational renewal. Without a fixed ideology to inherit or a party line to toe, younger leaders emerge on their own terms. They bring new perspectives. Their path to leadership depends on local engagement and integrity.

Institutionally, the model builds resilience through rules-not wishes. Measures such as omitting party names from ballots, directing state funding to individual candidates rather than parties, and banning formal whipping are not symbolic gestures. They are structural guardrails against political regression. By discouraging rigid party control, these rules ensure that collaboration remains open and adaptive-never calcified into permanent dominance.

Ultimately, the No-Party model's longevity lies in its honesty about power. It does not deny ambition, interest, or ideology. It merely denies them the right to monopolise the political stage. And in doing so, it lays the foundation for a democracy that can grow, renew, and defend itself—not through charisma or conformity, but through structure and consent.

Before concluding, it is important to clarify what this book is not proposing. We are not offering a rigid constitutional model to be copy-pasted across the world. We are not prescribing a particular electoral system, economic ideology, or form of statehood. Nations differ—in history, culture, structure, and political tradition—and so too must their democratic frameworks.

Some countries are parliamentary democracies, others presidential. Some operate under constitutional monarchies, like the United Kingdom, while others elect both heads of state and heads of government. Some nations use proportional representation systems that reward coalition-building. Others use majoritarian models like first-past-the-post, which tend to consolidate power into blocs. Some societies are committed to free-market capitalism. Others embrace social-democratic or socialist structures. Many fall somewhere in between.

We do not seek to overwrite any of these systems. We recognise their complexity, their cultural roots, and the local legitimacy they often carry. Our proposal is not about uniformity—it is about a core democratic upgrade that can be applied within any of these existing frameworks: removing party domination to make democracy more representative and accountable to the public.

We also acknowledge the deeper political and economic environments in which democracies exist. Systems of capitalism, globalisation, inequality, media control, and entrenched elites all shape the broader playing field. Some may rightly question whether a No-Party democracy could survive—let alone thrive—within such forces. But history shows us something revealing: party systems have not only failed across different conditions—they have often enabled that failure.

From Hitler's rise in Weimar Germany to Putin's consolidation of power in modern Russia, the pattern is unmistakable: leaders did not bypass the party system—they mastered it. Narendra Modi in India, Recep Tayyip Erdoğan in Turkey, Benjamin Netanyahu in Israel—all entrenched their rule through party machinery, not despite it. They used parties to centralise authority, suppress dissent, and cloak dominance in the language of democratic legitimacy. And they did so across vastly different cultural, economic, and constitutional landscapes. The lesson is clear: party systems are not safeguards against authoritarianism—they are often the very instruments that entrench it.

This is not to say that No-Party democracy is a flawless shield. No political structure is immune to human ambition, corruption, or inequality. But a No-Party system, by design, removes the permanent machinery that allows factional elites to entrench themselves in power. Without party infrastructure to hijack, representation resets with every election cycle—giving power back to voters, not factions.

No-Party democracy is not a final design. It is a flexible foundation. It can be adapted to suit a country's existing constitutional structure, economic system, and cultural expectations. What it insists upon is not uniformity—but authenticity. This flexibility allows each nation to build a model of self-government that reflects its character—while holding to the shared principle that power must serve the people.

Throughout history, every attempt to expand democratic participation has been met with resistance from those who benefit from the status quo. Monarchies feared republics. Landowners resisted suffrage. Segregationists denounced civil rights. The pattern is not new. What changes is the mechanism through which control is exercised—and today, that mechanism is the party system.

The institutions that claim to represent the people have long been engineered to manage them instead. Political parties do not merely contest elections—they organise power, enforce obedience, and mediate access to the political process. They are the final gatekeepers in systems that still describe themselves as free.

And those who benefit from this arrangement understand what is at stake. The emergence of a No-Party alternative—a system in which representatives are accountable to voters alone—poses a fundamental threat to the structure they have built. Their response is not confusion or ignorance. It is calculation. They will resist reform, not because it is unworkable, but because it is entirely workable—and because it works against them.

The tactics are familiar. Dismissals in the press. Ridicule from public intellectuals. Manufactured fears about instability, fragmentation, or extremism. Think tanks and media outlets—many funded by the same networks that bankroll political campaigns—will issue reports and warnings. Reformers will be painted as naïve, dangerous, or undemocratic. The language may change, but the purpose does not: to protect the system that protects them.

The intensity of their opposition does not reflect the weakness of No-Party democracy. It reflects the strength of its potential. Because once voters begin to understand that party loyalty is not an obligation, but a habit—once they see that the system is not fixed by nature but fixed by design—the illusion begins to break. And once it breaks, the task of maintaining it becomes exponentially harder.

Control then depends on noise—repetition, distraction, deflection. The goal is no longer to win a public argument, but to prevent one from happening. This is how elite power survives its crises: not by persuasion, but by managing the conditions under which ideas can be taken seriously.

The strength of No-Party democracy is not that it promises perfection. It is that it removes the structural barriers to accountability. It does not require extraordinary citizens. It requires a system that stops filtering representation through factions and loyalty structures. It assumes voters are capable of choosing candidates without needing a colour-coded cue. It allows politics to reflect what a society truly is—not what it is made to appear.

Yes, some independents will hold extreme or unpopular views. That is the nature of democratic exposure. But unlike today's parties, a No-Party system cannot hide such views behind a collective shield. It does not grant them institutional protection. It forces them into the open—where they must compete for public legitimacy on their own.

None of this means that change will come easily. Those who control systems rarely yield them voluntarily. Institutional inertia is powerful. And elite networks—corporate, media, political—will attempt to absorb, discredit, or delay anything that threatens their stability.

But history shows that once a structural shift gains traction, suppression becomes harder to sustain. When women demanded the right to vote, they were called anarchists. When apartheid fell, it was after decades of marginalisation and demonisation. The same resistance now faces those who challenge party rule—not because they are dangerous to democracy, but because they are dangerous to the power that speaks in democracy's name.

This is the moment of transition. The architecture of consent is cracking, and its defenders are responding—not with dialogue, but with denial.

The future remains unwritten. But one thing is increasingly clear: the legitimacy of party control is no longer taken for granted. And the more people recognise that representation can exist without it, the harder it becomes to defend.

By this stage, the conclusion should be self-evident: the party system does not merely fall short of its democratic promise—it actively obstructs it. Its purpose is no longer to organise public debate but to centralise political control, to convert participation into passive consent.

So the question is no longer what is broken. The question is how to respond.

This does not require revolution, but it does require disengagement—lawful, strategic, procedural. A shift in voting behaviour.

Millions protest unjust wars, rising inequality, and democratic decline, but as long as those same millions return to the ballot box and continue to validate the party system, the protests are neutralised. The system absorbs outrage—and continues.

In reality, the most effective way to challenge elite control in a functioning electoral system is not to shout louder, but to stop voting for the party machines that protect it. That decision—quiet, deliberate, and repeatable—is what changes everything.

The irony is hard to ignore: mass protest rarely translates into policy, yet even the angriest voters often cast ballots for the same party structures they denounce. Not because they agree with them—but because they feel trapped by the illusion of inevitability.

Yet there is an alternative. Not a utopia. Not a grand theory. Just a straightforward, peaceful act of refusal: vote for independents. Refuse to grant your consent to any party. Support candidates who are directly accountable to voters.

If millions of people—people who already oppose war, inequality, surveillance, and corporate impunity—began organising their voting behaviour not around ideologies, but around a single structural demand: independent representation, then the system begins to lose its grip. No march or petition can match that effect.

This is not fantasy. The electoral system still formally belongs to the electorate. As long as that remains true, the mechanism for structural change remains within reach—but only if people stop reinforcing the institutions that were built to contain them.

The moment voters begin to understand party politics not as a neutral organising principle, but as the primary mechanism by which elite interests are protected, the system begins to destabilise. Not violently. Not erratically. But procedurally—where it is most vulnerable.

This is the context in which the Coalition of Independents matters. It is not a party, nor an ideology, nor a movement based on loyalty. It is a platform for coordination—a way for unaffiliated candidates to work together to break the party monopoly using the only tool parties cannot fully capture: the vote.

It is a transitional strategy. It allows independent candidates—individuals who reject factional discipline and donor capture—to stand with clarity and coherence. They do not need to agree on every issue. What binds them is structural: their authority flows from their constituents alone.

Public feeling, when organised, can achieve extraordinary leverage. Across democratic systems, insurgent movements—from the Brexit Party in the UK to the Five Star Movement in Italy, and independent presidential campaigns in the US—have forced ruling elites to respond. These movements didn't need to govern for decades to make an impact. Their strength lay in disruption: shifting the debate, exposing vulnerabilities, and compelling establishment concessions. The same principle applies here: once independent candidates gain electoral traction, parties are forced into reaction. The illusion of control weakens.

And once a few independents are elected—and demonstrate that they are not only viable but effective—momentum builds. Confidence grows. Others come forward. As awareness spreads among the public, so too does the speed of transformation. The more voters recognise that real representation is possible without parties, the more rapidly the old system loses its hold. With time, those elected without party affiliation gain enough leverage to propose structural reforms that parties would never enact voluntarily, such as:

- **The removal of party names from ballots**
- **The elimination of public funding for political parties**
- **The removal of legal recognition or privileges granted to parties as corporate entities**
- **A review of parliamentary rules that favour party blocs over individual representatives**

These are not abstract demands. They are practical changes designed to neutralise the machinery of party control—not to suppress political views, but to prevent their monopolisation.

This is how structural change begins: not with slogans, but with disobedience at the ballot box. Not with permission, but with quiet refusal. The party system depends on a public that continues to vote for it, even after recognising its failures. The moment enough people say, "we will vote—but not for you," its legitimacy collapses.

The greatest illusion in modern politics is the belief that power cannot be challenged. That no alternative exists. That participation means picking between options already chosen for you. This illusion produces passivity—not because people don't care, but because they believe nothing can be done.

But the tools for change are already available. No permission is needed. No institution must first approve. If just a fraction of disillusioned citizens—the same ones who fill the streets, sign petitions, or withdraw in protest—chose to vote only for independents, the balance would begin to shift. If that fraction became a pattern, and that pattern became a principle, the system would begin to unravel—from the inside.

So the question must be asked clearly: If not this—then what? Is there a more effective, more peaceful, more legally sound method for disrupting elite control than electing people who owe the system nothing? Is there a more direct way to strip influence from party donors, lobbyists, and political operatives than refusing to vote for any structure they can capture?

If another option exists, it has yet to be articulated. And if it does not, then this is not just a viable strategy—it is a necessary one.

The law does not require party loyalty. The ballot does not exclude independents. The only thing preventing change is the belief that change is not possible.

The Coalition of Independents is not a brand. It is not a personality cult. It is a tool—a structure designed to help voters and candidates organise around the principle of No-Party democracy. Nothing more, nothing less.

It also does not guarantee perfection. A No-Party system will still reflect the divisions, prejudices, and contradictions present in society itself. Some candidates will be principled. Others may not be. Some may represent deeply conservative, religious, or even intolerant views—just as they do now. The difference is that, in a No-Party system, those views are no longer sanitised by party branding. There is no collective shield to hide behind. Every candidate stands for what they are—and every voter is forced to confront the reality of what they are endorsing.

That is the point. No-Party democracy does not create a better society. It exposes the one that already exists. It replaces illusion with responsibility. It ensures that accountability cannot be outsourced to a manifesto or excused by party compromise. The system becomes transparent—not perfect, but honest.

In a world where cruelty and corruption are often rewarded, it is easy to believe that most people are inherently selfish, indifferent, or tribal. But history tells us otherwise. Across every nation and generation, there are always those who choose to do what is right, even when no one is watching.

Writer and cultural critic Susan Sontag once observed that 10% of any population will be cruel no matter what, and 10% will be merciful no matter what. The remaining 80% will follow the examples set by those in charge. This observation speaks volumes. It tells us that human beings are malleable—that most people are neither monsters nor saints, but simply conform to what society rewards or punishes. When cruelty is normalized and rewarded, most become complicit or indifferent. But when kindness, justice, and truth are the standards, most people will reflect those values instead.

The question, then, is not whether humanity can change. The question is: Who is shaping the moral compass of our societies?

Today, the cruel and calculating 10% hold the reins of global power. They do not rise through wisdom, compassion, or public service, but through loyalty to entrenched interests, obedience to elite agendas, and a ruthless willingness to betray the common good for private gain. These are not leaders in any true sense—they are functionaries of empire, architects of war, defenders of inequality, and manipulators of fear. Cloaked in patriotic slogans, they sell cruelty as strength and obedience as virtue.

The party system—once imagined as a tool of democratic representation—has become a machinery of managed consent. From East to West, it has enabled elites to centralize control while maintaining the illusion of choice. In the USSR, the Communist Party became not the vanguard of the people, but an imperial apparatus of repression—swallowing nations and silencing dissent in the name of "progress." In the West, party machines unleashed the First and Second World Wars, killing over 100 million people, maiming countless more, and redrawing the world through carnage and conquest.

But the story isn't as simple as East bad, West worse. History demands more nuance. For centuries before the Cold War, Western colonial empires—Britain, France, Spain, Portugal, the Netherlands—looted, enslaved, and devastated vast swaths of Asia, Africa, and the Americas. India, once one of the world's richest civilizations, was drained into poverty under British rule. China was dismembered by opium and gunboats. Entire continents were turned into extraction zones for European capital.

The rise of the Soviet Union, whatever its internal contradictions, broke that monopoly. It rivalled the West not just with ideology, but with guns, training, and political support that altered the balance of global power. In Cuba, Soviet backing enabled Fidel Castro to nationalize U.S. sugar plantations and defy the Monroe Doctrine. In Vietnam, Soviet weapons and advisors helped Ho Chi Minh's forces defeat both French colonialists and the U.S. military. In Angola and Mozambique, Soviet-aligned guerrillas drove out Portuguese colonizers in the 1970s. Algeria threw off the French and reclaimed its oil and gas—not by appealing to Western diplomacy, but by taking power through armed resistance, often with Soviet assistance.

These victories were not perfect, and many new regimes became authoritarian. But they ended centuries of direct colonial domination, and for the first time in modern history, resource-rich nations began reclaiming control over their own land.

That world is now being violently reversed. Today's conflicts are not just about ideology—they are about restoring extractive dominance under new banners: "human rights," "security," "rules-based order." Ukraine is the most visible frontline—not just for its geography or the trillions in rare earth minerals beneath its soil, but because it is a keystone in a larger imperial strategy. The war serves multiple objectives: weakening Russia, containing China, expanding NATO's reach, and reasserting Western control over Eurasia. Ukraine's natural wealth is seen not as a national inheritance, but as a prize to be opened for foreign investment and postwar contracts.

And Ukraine is only one theatre. Georgia, Moldova, and Taiwan are already entangled in similar games of pressure and provocation. Wherever there are resources to extract, borders to weaponize, or influence to project, the imperial logic resurfaces—rebranded but unchanged.

The most dangerous aspect of today's imperial order is its invisibility. Expansionism no longer marches under a single flag—it moves through the machinery of mainstream politics. From Washington to Brussels, so-called democracies follow the same script: endless wars, deregulated markets, and absolute impunity for the powerful. This isn't conspiracy—it's structure. The system doesn't care what mask it wears: left or right, green or gold, dove or hawk. Beneath every label is the same machinery—advancing profit, power, and control at any human cost.

Presidents and prime ministers are largely powerless against this machinery—not because they lack formal authority, but because they are almost always products of the system itself. By the time they reach high office, they have been vetted, co-opted, or conditioned to serve entrenched interests. Those who attempt to step outside those boundaries—who challenge the intelligence establishment, the military-industrial complex, or the financial elite—are marginalized, discredited, or in some cases, eliminated—like President John F. Kennedy.

Donald Trump campaigned as a populist outsider—a critic of endless wars and entrenched elites. But once in office, he became yet another steward of empire. In 2025, he launched direct air and naval strikes on Houthi forces in Yemen, killing civilians and escalating an already devastating conflict. Months later, he authorized major bombing raids on Iranian nuclear sites, using bunker-busting munitions in an unprecedented pre-emptive strike.

Despite promising to "drain the swamp," he filled his cabinet with Wall Street insiders and neoconservatives—and despite pledging transparency, he failed to release the Epstein files, protecting the very networks his base believed he would expose. His presidency became a case study in how even so-called outsiders are absorbed, neutralized, or repurposed by the machinery they claim to oppose.

The real decisions are made by unelected actors: intelligence agencies, military contractors, financial institutions, supranational bodies, and media conglomerates that shape not just policy, but public perception. Presidents preside; they do not rule. The public, fed a constant diet of fear, scandal, and division, is invited to vote—but never to choose.

As long as we continue to participate in this theater—religiously voting for and identifying with one brand of the same corrupted machine over another—we validate our own manipulation.

To escape this trap, we must stop being partisan spectators and start becoming conscious participants. The real conflict is no longer between left and right, East and West, or even democracy and authoritarianism—it is between the people and the machine that feeds on them. A machine that thrives on division, profits from fear, and, if left unchecked, will drive us toward a final, global catastrophe.

If we do not reject the terms set for us—if we do not dismantle the machine rather than vote to oil its gears—then we remain complicit in its destruction: of nations, of democracy, and perhaps of civilization itself.

But Sontag's insight offers hope. There is always another 10%—the merciful. These are the ones who cannot turn a blind eye. They are the voices of conscience: those who speak truth under pressure, who act with integrity even when it isolates them, who show compassion where cruelty prevails. They may come from any background—diplomats, doctors, dissidents, or ordinary witnesses. They may not be perfect, but they are principled, consistently acting out of compassion and justice, even at great personal cost.

If this merciful 10% rises—if they organize and awaken to their collective power—they can inspire the 80% to change what is normal, what is politically acceptable, and what is possible. When the merciful lead with courage, the silent majority will follow. And when that happens, the entrenched cruelty of the elite will no longer have the power to hold society in place.

What if government were not in the hands of party loyalists—who, today, are predominantly from the 10% cruel section—but of independent citizens, many of whom would come from the merciful 10%? What if the majority of elected representatives embodied compassion, justice, and truth? What if decisions were not shaped by donors and lobbyists, but by transparent assemblies of public representatives free from party pressure? What if the norms of society were set by those who prioritize kindness, justice, and human dignity?

That world is not a fantasy—it is a political possibility. It begins when the merciful 10% recognize their responsibility—not just to feel or protest, but to lead. To abandon party systems that reward conformity and cruelty, and to champion a new democratic model—one based on independent representation, radical accountability, and shared humanity.

When they do, the 80% will not resist them—they will follow. And when that happens, even the cruelty of the entrenched elite will no longer be enough to hold the world in place.

History is not made by majorities. It is made by minorities of conviction who shape the rules others live by. The cruel 10% have ruled long enough, through violence, deception, and manipulation. But if the merciful 10% rise up—with clarity, courage, and vision—they can lead the silent majority into a new era. One not dictated by parties, but by people. Not shaped by fear, but by fairness. Not ruled by the powerful, but guided by the just.

Once enough people act on this principle, the effects become irreversible. A few independents can break the echo chamber. A few dozen can reshape the debate. A critical mass can dismantle the legal scaffolding that keeps parties in power.

But none of it will happen unless people step forward—not as spectators, not as cynics, not as partisans—but as active, engaged citizens.

Everyone has a role to play. Whether you are a voter, a candidate, a teacher, a journalist, a student, a business owner, or simply a concerned member of the public—your refusal to legitimize the party system is a political act. Your choice to vote for an independent is not merely symbolic. It is structural. And when enough people make that same choice, the system changes—not by force, but by design.

Democracy began as a noble idea—born in philosophy, raised in revolution—but it entered history in chains, constrained from the start by those who feared its true potential. More than just a system of government, democracy is a philosophy of empowerment—a belief in the inherent dignity and agency of every individual. From the ancient agora of Athens to the public squares of modern states, the struggle for democracy has been shaped by conflict, sacrifice, and the relentless pursuit of justice.

Its moral appeal is undeniable: the conviction that everyone, regardless of their station, deserves an equal say in the decisions that shape society. This belief runs deep in our collective consciousness, fueling our continued reverence for democratic ideals.

Through the act of voting, citizens are meant to exercise their sovereignty—choosing representatives to speak and act on their behalf. It is this ideal—the representation of the people's will—that has made democracy the most enduring and admired form of governance across generations.

The party system has become its greatest restraint. Though not born of democratic philosophy, the party system has been woven into it—not to unite us, but to sort, separate, and turn us against one another. It thrives on conflict, on false choices, and on the illusion of representation.

The only way democracy can be freed is if we—the people—refuse to be led by institutions that have never truly served us. The system will not fall through protest or outrage. It will not be saved by a new party or a charismatic leader. It will collapse when we stop feeding it—when we stop voting for any party, when we withdraw our consent, our participation, and our belief in its legitimacy.

Only then can democracy, at last, become what it was always meant to be—in the words of Abraham Lincoln, "government of the people, by the people, for the people."

About the Author

METIN PEKIN earned his BA (Hons) in Political Economy from the University of Greenwich before embarking on a career as a serial entrepreneur, founding and growing multiple companies from the ground up. Building businesses over decades gave him direct experience of how economic power translates into political power. Combining his academic background with hard-won experience, Pekin began to see a troubling pattern: in every election, regardless of which party won, the same outcomes repeated. Inequality deepened, mass surveillance expanded, whistleblowers were punished, and wars continued. Genuine reformers were sidelined, and party gatekeepers decided who could even compete for power. *Breaking Democracy's Chains* is his first book, a deeply researched case for why the only solution is to break the grip of political parties altogether, finally creating genuine democracy and returning power to the people.

www.ingramcontent.com/pod-product-compliance
Lightning Source LLC
LaVergne TN
LVHW041629060526
838200LV00040B/1507